‖‖‖ ‖‖‖‖‖‖‖‖‖‖‖‖‖‖‖‖‖‖‖‖‖‖‖‖‖‖‖
W9-AGZ-667

597.8   Fridell, Ron.
FRI
         Amphibians in
         danger.

                                    24475

$25.00

DATE			

597.8   NASHOBA REGIONAL HIGH SCHOOL
FRI
         Amphibians in danger.

‖‖‖‖‖‖‖‖‖‖‖‖‖‖‖‖‖‖‖‖‖‖‖
24475

BAKER & TAYLOR

AMPHIBIANS IN DANGER

A WORLDWIDE WARNING

By Ron Fridell

Franklin Watts
A Division of Grolier Publishing
New York • London • Hong Kong • Sydney
Danbury, Connecticut

Photographs ©: Biological Photo Service: 26 (Ed Ely); David Leibman: 30; Gamma-Liaison: 65 (Marcel Ehrhard), 73 (Cynthia Johnson), 29 (Dale C. Spartas); Greenpeace: 50, 58 (Salem Krieger); Joan Fellers: 63; Michael & Patricia Fogden: 8; Minnesota Pollution Control Agency: 60; Oregon State University: 35 (Andrew Blaustein); Peter Arnold Inc.: 53 (Drs. Kessel & Shih), 6 (Hans Pfletschinger), 5 (Kevin Schafer); Photo Researchers: 39 (Sally Bensusen/SPL), 16 (A. Cosmos Blank), back cover (Jeff Lepore), 10 (Tom McHugh), 17 (John Mitchell); Tony Stone Images: cover (K. Schafer/M. Hill); U.S. Department of Interior: 22; University of California: 14 (Saxon Donnelly); University of Georgia, Savannha River Ecology Lab: 46; University of Minnesota, Twin Cities Campus: 55; Visuals Unlimited: 11 (Robert Clay), 43 (Rob Simpson).
Insert #1 photographs ©: Biological Photo Service: 2 (Ed Ely); Charles Drost: 3; Michael & Patricia Fogden: 1, 5; Peter Arnold Inc.: 11 (R. Andrew Odue); Photo Researchers: 4, 12 (Stephen Dalton), 6 (Anthony Mercieca), 8 (Steinhart Aquarium); Steven Holt/Aigrette Photography: 7; The Image Works: 9 (John Eastcott/Yva Momatiuk); Wolfgang Käehler: 10.
Insert #2 photographs ©: Biological Photo Service: 2 (David J. Wrobel); Dr. Scott P. McRobert, Director of Biodiversity Lab, St. Joseph University: 9, 10; Gary Braasch: 1; Photo Researchers: 3 (Suzanne L. Collins), 5, 7 (Suzanne L. & Joseph T. Collins), 6 (Joseph T. Collins), 8 (M. P. Gadomski), 11 (C. K. Lorenz); Steven Holt/Aigrette Photography: 4; Visuals Unlimited: 12 (A. Kerstitch); Wyoming Game & Fish Dept.: 13 (Cody Beers).

Book design by Joan M. McEvoy

Library of Congress Cataloging-in-Publication Data

Fridell, Ron
    Amphibians in danger: a worldwide warning/ Ron Fridell.
        p. cm.
    Includes bibliographical references and index.
    Summary: Describes the alarming worldwide disapearence of amphibians and its possible link to such conditions as erosion of the ozone layer, greenhouse effect and global warming, and environmental pollution.
    ISBN 0-531-11373-5
    1. Amphibians—Monitoring—Juvenile literature.   2. Endangered species—Juvenile literature. 1. Amphibians. 2. Endangered species.] I. Title.
QL644.2.F75 1999
597.8'168—dc21
                                                                    98-39163
                                                                    CIP
                                                                    AC

© 1999 by Ron Fridell
All rights reserved. Published simultaneously in Canada.
Printed in the United States of America.
1 2 3 4 5 6 7 8 9 10 R 08 07 06 05 04 03 02 01 00 99

CONTENTS

NASHOBA REGIONAL HIGH SCHOOL
MEDIA CENTER

INTRODUCTION
EARLY WARNINGS

In 1973, Cynthia Carey was a student at the University of Colorado. She was studying the Western toad in the nearby Elk Mountains. Carey was very fond of these toads. "They have beautiful eyes. You can really fall in love with them," she said.[1]

Twice a week she would head out into the Colorado wilderness to observe these wart-covered, 4-inch (10-cm) long creatures. On one trip—a trip she will never forget—she initially had trouble finding the toads. She was puzzled. They'd always been easy to spot before—abundant and lively, hopping everywhere.

"I was sad and mystified," said Carey as she recalled that day.[2] Dozens of toads lay in the grass. Some were barely moving; others were not moving at all. The toads seemed to be suffering from red leg disease, an infectious illness that causes internal bleeding. As a result, the toads' legs look red and puffy.

Red leg disease is a bacterial infection that can also affect fish and humans. The *bacteria* that cause the illness are common in freshwater lakes and ponds. They can remain inactive within a toad's body for long periods of time. When an infected toad experiences a stressful event, the bacteria may become active. Carey had seen red leg disease before, but this was different. Red leg disease usually wasn't fatal. Why were these toads dying?

Countless Western toads like this one have vanished from the mountains of Colorado.

Carey picked up one of the dead toads and brought it back to the University of Colorado. A veterinarian examined the toad and confirmed that it had died of red leg disease. The toad had died for the same reason that a human infected with *HIV* dies of strep throat or pneumonia. Its *immune system* had shut down, so the toad couldn't fight the infection.

Now Carey had another question. What had caused the toad's immune system to fail? The toads she was studying lived in a protected wilderness area. There were no highways, houses, or factories belching toxic smoke nearby. No one had poisoned the water or sprayed the mountain slopes with *pesticides*. Why had the immune systems of all those toads collapsed so suddenly and so completely?

Another Sign of Trouble

Meanwhile, halfway around the world, an eerily similar biological mystery was unfolding. It focused on one of Earth's truly unique amphibians—the gastric brooding frog of the Conandale and Blackall mountains in Queensland, Australia.

What made gastric brooders unique? They didn't reproduce like other frogs. Most female frogs lay their eggs in the water, usually in a pond or stream. After the eggs are laid, the males fertilize them and then both parents go their separate ways. Neither parent watches over or cares for the eggs.

MY HOW YOU'VE CHANGED

During puberty, we humans go through substantial physical changes. We transform from children to adults. But the changes we go through are nothing compared to what a frog goes through as it changes from a tadpole to an adult frog.

A frog begins its life as an egg. It is one of many eggs in a jellylike mass laid by its mother and fertilized by its father. The mass floats along on the surface of a pond or stream. If it isn't eaten by a fish, turtle, or some other *predator*, the eggs will hatch.

These tadploes have recently hatched from eggs.

A tadpole has an oval head and a long slender tail. It breathes through gill slits. As the tadpole grows, amazing changes take place. It develops hind legs, and then front legs. Soon, its tail vanishes. Eventually, the tadpole's gills disappear and it begins to breathe with lungs. The tadpole's *metamorphosis* is now complete. It has become a froglet—a miniature version of its parents and of the frog it will soon become.

Gastric brooders did things differently. After the male fertilized the eggs, the female swallowed them. While the eggs incubated in her stomach, the female shut down her digestive system and didn't eat anything. Because the eggs hatched in her stomach, the tadpoles were safe from predators. After the tadpoles had metamorphosed into froglets, the female opened her mouth and spit them out into the world, one by one.

Gastric brooders had other fascinating habits, too. While in the water, they sat in small groups and touched one another's front fingers, as if holding hands. On land, they lay on their backs with all four feet in the air and basked in the narrow streams of sunlight that shone through the thick canopy to the forest floor.

At one time, these fascinating creatures were so abundant that a researcher could easily observe 100 in a single night. But in 1973—the same year that Cynthia Carey discovered the dead and dying Western toads in Colorado—gastric brooders began disappearing from their well-protected *rain forest* habitat. By 1981, the gastric brooders in Australia had vanished forever and the Western toads in Colorado were on the brink of *extinction*, and hardly anyone seemed to notice.

The Trend Continues

A few years later, the same mysterious fate befell another amphibian. This time it was the golden toad of Costa Rica, a creature whose absence the world could not help but notice. This brilliant 2-inch (5-cm) amphibian had turned into a worldwide tourist attraction for the mountainous Monteverde Cloud Forest Reserve. The reserve, which is located 5,000 feet (1,524 m) above sea level, was the golden toad's only known habitat.

While we generally think of toads as dull, brownish-gray creatures, golden toads were so bright and shiny that they mesmerized scientists. According to one, they looked as if they'd been dipped in enamel paint. Another researcher called them tiny jewels on the forest floor. The males shone a brilliant gold, while the females sported scarlet spots ringed with yellow on a jet-black background.

These golden toads (*Bufo periglenes*) thrived in the Costa Rican rain forest before mysteriously disappearing in 1990.

These toads appeared to spend nearly all their lives underground, emerging only to breed. Males gathered in pools of water, waiting for females to emerge and mate with them. Afterward, the females laid 200 to 400 eggs, each the size of a teardrop, in a long string. Golden toads laid so many eggs because very few offspring survived to adulthood.

In April and May 1987, scientists counted approximately 1,500 golden toads at the Brillante ponds, the toads' primary breeding site on the Monteverde Reserve. Then something happened. During the next 2 years, they saw only one golden toad at the site. In 1990, they saw none at all. Another amphibian *species* living in a well-protected habitat had vanished. It wasn't long before scientists began to realize that amphibian populations were *declining* all over the world.

CHAPTER 1
A LOOK AT AMPHIBIANS

What Are Amphibians?

Amphibians can be divided into three groups: the *anurans*, salamanders, and *caecilians*. Anurans—frogs and toads— are the most common type of amphibian. There are about 4,000 known species of anurans. Most of them live in tropical climates, but some are found as far north as the Arctic Circle and as far south as the southern tip of South America. All anurans have four legs. They use their long hind legs for jumping. Because a toad's skin is thicker and less moist than a frog's, a toad can tolerate drier conditions than a frog.

Most salamanders have four legs, but a few kinds have just two legs. All salamanders have a long tail. Some salamanders have a special protective strategy. Their tail breaks off if a predator bites it. This distracts the enemy long enough for the salamander to escape. Later, the salamander grows a new tail. Salamanders can also grow new legs. There are about 360 known species of salamanders. They live in temperate zones, where there are significant changes in temperature from season to season. Salamanders are also found in warm, humid areas of Central and South America.

Caecilians have no legs at all. They look like overgrown earthworms. There are about 160 known species of caecilians. Most live in underground burrows in tropical regions of the world, but a few species live in the water.

With their wormlike bodies, caecilians make excellent burrowers.

Our View of Amphibians

Historically, people have never been too fond of amphibians. We think of them as squat, laughably ugly creatures. They can't soar like eagles, sprint like cheetahs, trumpet like elephants, or swing through the trees like chimpanzees. They aren't cute and cuddly like a koala bear or a puppy, either. Except for *Sesame Street's* Kermit the Frog, we just don't see amphibians as lovable creatures.

Most people tend to rate toads even lower than frogs. They have warty-looking skin, and some people still believe the old myth about getting warts from handling toads. Many toads have glands that secrete *toxins*. These poisons can make you sick if they get into your mouth. Some salamanders produce toxins, too. One rough-skinned newt makes enough toxin to kill 25,000 white mice!

Among the long list of people who see amphibians as foul, loathsome creatures was Carolus Linnaeus, a brilliant eighteenth-century naturalist. Linnaeus developed a system for identifying, classifying, and naming living things based on their physical appearance and patterns of behavior. Most modern scientists still use his system to organize creatures into groups.

The rough-skinned newt
(*Taricha granulosa*)

SCIENTIFIC NAMES

Why do scientists give animal species strange-sounding names? It all started in the eighteenth century when a Swedish naturalist named Carolus Linnaeus developed a system for classifying all living things. At that time, all educated people learned Latin as well as their own language. Linnaeus used Latin words to name living things so that no matter where scientists lived or what language they spoke, they would all call creatures by the same names. A scientific name consists of two words and is always italicized. The first letter of the first word is capitalized, and the first letter of the second word is lowercased.

For example, the scientific name for human beings is *Homo sapiens*. In Latin, "homo" means "human being," and "sapiens" means "intelligent." Most scientific names tell you something about the creature. Can you guess what *Tyrannosaurus rex* means? In Latin, "tyrannosaurus" means "tyrant lizard," and "rex " means "king."

Each species is named by the scientist who first describes it. Here are a few of the scientific names of amphibians you'll see in this book and what they mean in Latin.

Bufo boreas = Bufo (a toad) + boreas (the north wind)
Rana muscosa = Rana (a frog) + muscosa (fly, mosquito)
Bufo calamita = Bufo (a toad) + calamita (loss, misfortune)
Rana cascadea = Rana (a frog) + cascadea (Cascade Mountains in Oregon)

As you might guess, *Rana cascadea* live in the Cascade Mountains. This name is one example of how scientists sometimes create names by "Latinizing" words from other languages. This is often done when a scientific name includes the name of a place or a person. Can you guess who the giant ground sloth *Megalonyx jeffersonii* was named after? Here's a hint—he was the third president of the United States.

Luckily, not all scientists agree with Linnaeus. Cynthia Carey is just one of the many researchers who respect amphibians. These scientists see amphibians as unique, hardy creatures. Amphibians have been living on Earth for about 350 million years. Well over 4,000 species of amphibians live in habitats all over the world today. They are the only group of animals on Earth that lead a double life—they spend part of their lives on land and part in the water. Amphibians are real survivors.

Although amphibians have inhabited Earth at least three times longer than humans, their future is now uncertain. The Western toad *(Bufo boreas)* has virtually disappeared, and the gastric brooding frog *(Rhobatrachus silus)* and golden toad *(Bufo periglenes)* are already gone. How many other species will follow?

A Worldwide Problem

In 1989, David Wake, director of the Museum of *Vertebrate* Zoology at the University of California at Berkeley, was studying the mountain yellow-legged frog, *Rana muscosa*. This frog is common to the Sierra Nevada mountains of central and northern California. Wake had been conducting research at sites in these mountains since 1959, and considered them a haven for *herpetologists*—scientists who study reptiles and amphibians.

In the summer of 1989, Wake and his students were deeply disturbed by what they found at their study sites. In the past, mountain yellow-legged frogs had been so abundant that the scientists had to be careful not to step on them. That year, the frogs were few and far between.

When Wake shared his bad news with other scientists at the first World Congress of Herpetology in Canterbury, England, he realized right away that he'd hit a nerve. One after another, concerned scientists came to him with their own alarming stories of amphibian decline.

- In Oregon, the population of the frog *Rana cascadea* had declined by 80 percent.

David Wake is a leader in the fight to protect amphibians in danger.

- In Reserva Atlantica, Brazil, the diurnal hylodine frog, known for its eerie birdlike calls, had disappeared.
- In El Yunque, the Puerto Rican rain forest, *Eleutherodactylus jasperi*—a frog that once gave birth to live young—was now extinct.
- On the slopes of Volcán Tajumulco, Guatemala's highest mountain, seven species of salamanders had disappeared.
- In the cloud forests of the Andes Mountains in Ecuador and Venezuela, eight species of frogs had vanished.

The list went on and on. Species after species of amphibians was declining, *endangered*, or extinct. In Great Britain, it was the natterjack toad (*Bufo calamita*); in southern California, it was the arroyo toad. In Costa Rica, the brightly colored harlequin frog (*Atelopus varius*) had vanished from the very same habitat where the golden toad once lived.

Wake knew many of the world's amphibians were in trouble, but he had no idea of the scope of the problem until he heard from all the scientists at the World Congress. This wasn't just a local phenomenon; something was killing amphibians all over the planet. No one knew why they were dying, how to stop the killing, or what the killing might ultimately mean for the species known as *Homo sapiens*.

Why We Need Amphibians

Amphibians are a vital part of the Earth's *biodiversity*—the variety of species on the planet. Few groups of animals come in as many different species and have as many different lifestyles as amphibians. Amphibians live in almost every type of *habitat* on Earth. The species living in different parts of the world have developed in ways that make them well suited for their environment.

The now extinct gastric brooders, which incubated their eggs in their stomachs and spit out their offspring, are very different from tiger tree frogs (*Phyllomedusa hypocondrialis*), which raise up their entire bodies and walk with slow, deliberate steps like little amphibian robots. Both of these frogs are quite different from glass frogs, which have skin so thin and clear that you can actually see their internal organs working. The female Surinam toad carries her eggs in envelopes of soft skin on her back until the young pop out as toadlets. The yellow-legged tadpole is able to delay its own development up to 2 years if the weather in its surroundings is too cold for it to survive as an adult. When any species of amphibian dies off, Earth's biodiversity decreases. The result is a poorer, less stable, less predictable environment for every living thing—ourselves included.

Amphibians also form a vital link in Earth's *food web*, as both predators and *prey*. As predators, they provide a far safer and simpler method than pesticides for controlling insect populations. Amphibians are highly efficient pest-control machines and are fascinating to observe in action. Most frogs, for example, have long sticky tongues that they flick lightning-fast to snatch flying insects out of the air. After a frog catches a victim, it shuts its eyelids tight. This action presses the frog's eyeballs down into the roof of its mouth, helping to force the food down its throat.

Frogs and toads consume countless agricultural pests and biting insects. Take mosquitoes, for instance. Asian nations that export vast

A frog snatching its
next meal

numbers of frogs to Europe for human consumption (Yes, people really do eat frogs.) find that their mosquito populations are skyrocketing, and that they must depend more and more on expensive pesticides. In 1987, India actually banned the export of frogs for human consumption after finding that two species of bullfrogs were close to extinction.

As prey, amphibians serve as a vital source of food for many mammals, reptiles, birds, and fish. Some of these animals eat only adults, while others feed on eggs or tadpoles or both. When amphibians are removed from the food web, everything changes—for the worse.

Amphibians also contribute directly to our well-being. In fact, millions of frogs and toads have died for human benefit. Most American schoolchildren dissect a frog in biology class to learn firsthand about an animal's inner workings. Research on African clawed frogs has helped researchers develop cures for the crippling effects of cystic fibrosis and Parkinson's disease. For centuries, the Chinese have used ch'an su, a powder made from toad skin, to treat heart problems. Scientists have used the venomous South American poison dart frog in the production of ABT-594, a potent painkiller for cancer patients. ABT-594 appears to

The blue-bellied poison dart frog (*Epipedobates azuri-ventris*)

be as effective as morphine, but is not addictive. As amphibian species disappear, so do potential cures for human illnesses.

POISON FROG AND TOAD LEGENDS

Every animal has stories associated with it, some of them ancient. Certain of these ancient stories are based on fact; others are pure fantasy—and sometimes it's hard to tell which is which. As you learned earlier, some toads and frogs are poisonous. Their skin secretes toxins that may be harmful, or even fatal. Here are some stories *anthropologists* have heard about the power of poison toads and frogs.

- To acquire "hunting magic," rain-forest hunters make ointment from poisonous frogs. During an all-night ceremony, these hunter-warriors burn their own skin, then rub a stick coated with the poisonous frog ointment onto the burns. The next morning they are supposed to be stronger and more alert.
- These same hunter-warriors rub arrow tips and darts across a poisonous toad's or frog's back. According to legend, the poison is so powerful that even a minor wound from a poisoned arrow or dart is fatal to the enemy.
- Secretions produced by a certain kind of frog are said to change the color of a parrot's feathers. It works this way: You pull one of the parrot's feathers out and rub some secretion from the frog on the spot. When a new feather grows in, it will be a different color.
- Some people say that if you rub a frog on your wounds, the toxins on its skin will heal your wounds.

Whether you believe these legends or not, they show that frogs and toads play a powerful part in some people's lives.

Amphibians are also important simply because they are creatures of Earth, just like us. They have a right to exist. If humans are responsible for amphibian decline—and it appears that we are—then we have a responsibility to protect the amphibians that are still alive.

Perhaps the best reason to be concerned about amphibians—at least from a selfish point of view—is to protect ourselves. According to David Wake, "Frogs are in essence a messenger."[1] Their decline is a warning to us all. Their extinction could lead to the extinction of other species and, eventually, to the extinction of all species.

Chapter 2
Mysterious Messages

Scientists attend professional conferences for two reasons: to catch up on the latest news in their field and to meet and talk with one another. During the day, scientists present papers about their research and discuss the results. In the evening, they have dinner together. As they eat, they share all the latest gossip and find out about current job openings. When the conference is over, everyone goes home and focuses their attention on their own research projects.

The first World Congress of Herpetology in 1989 was different. David Wake and other scientists were extremely concerned to discover that declining amphibian populations were a worldwide problem. They organized an emergency conference to deal with this specific issue.

The 2-day emergency conference took place at the University of California at Irvine in February 1990. The day was beautiful, but the forty people at the conference weren't paying any attention to the weather outside. They spent their time in a windowless room discussing their concerns. When Wake decided who to invite to the conference, he'd looked for people with many different points of view. There were herpetologists, *ecologists*, members of wildlife conservation groups, and officials from scientific organizations.

The participants listened as each person described his or her experiences. They learned about amphibian declines in Germany, Wyoming, Costa Rica, Australia, Panama, Great Britain, California, Canada, Switzerland, Japan, Norway, and other places. It was soon apparent to everyone that amphibians all over the world were in trouble. Why were the participants so concerned about this worldwide amphibian decline? The answers lie at the very heart of what amphibians are.

Like Canaries in Coal Mines

With no scales, hair, or feathers to protect them, amphibians have more intimate contact with the environment than other animals do. They take in air and moisture through their thin, *permeable* skin, which readily absorbs chemicals from soil and water.

Amphibians are also exposed to more environments and more parts of any given environment than many other creatures. They can be found on every continent except Antarctica, and live in all sorts of places—from deserts to forests and from deep valleys to mountaintops. Most adult amphibians spend time on land and in the water. In addition, amphibians feed at different points on the food web at different times in their life. As tadpoles, they consume plant matter; as adults, they eat insects.

Zoologist Henry Wilbur of Duke University has compared amphibians to canaries in coal mines. In the past, coal miners brought canaries with them into mine shafts. These small birds have delicate respiratory systems, so they are much more sensitive to toxic gases than people are. When a canary had trouble breathing—or died—miners knew the shaft was not safe and hurried to the surface. Amphibians are our canaries—they act as environmental monitors.

This is not to say that amphibians are not also hardy survivors. They've been around for hundreds of millions of years longer than we have. They survived whatever changes wiped out about 90 percent of all ocean species 250 million years ago. They lived through whatever forces drove the mighty dinosaurs to extinction 65 million years ago. We don't know exactly what caused the major extinctions of the past, but we do

William Brown of the U.S. Department of the Interior

know that human activities are currently changing Earth's environment more rapidly than whatever caused the earlier extinctions.

These changes may be happening so fast that amphibians, and other creatures, cannot adapt quickly enough to survive. William Brown, science adviser to the secretary of the interior, sees it this way: "When species like frogs and toads that have been with us since the Jurassic period suddenly start to disappear—without us understanding exactly why—you have to take notice."[1]

Putting a Plan in Action

Wake and other scientists attending the 1990 emergency conference at Irvine suspected that the widespread declines in amphibian populations could be a signal of a worldwide environmental emergency. They proposed that the problems amphibians were encountering with survival might well indicate problems that humans would sooner or later encounter.

The researchers knew that they didn't have enough data to prove that they were right, so they discussed the best way to collect that data. Some suggested conducting surveys—going to places all over the world and counting the number of amphibians. Others thought that entire *ecosystems* should be studied. That meant selecting specific sites—such as ponds or marshes—and monitoring amphibians, insects, birds, fish, mammals, and plant life as well as studying the relationships among them.

Their most pressing problem, they agreed, was a lack of organization. No single institution was willing to take the lead in the effort to save endangered amphibians. This, Wake said, was the primary reason that no one had recognized the magnitude of the problem until the first World Congress of Herpetology.

Everyone at the emergency conference knew that the situation would have to change, and fast. Time was running out. They realized they would have to create their own organization—an international working group that would conduct a worldwide scientific investigation of amphibian decline.

Creating the group was easier said than done. As persistent and dedicated as he was, it took David Wake nearly 2 years to get the group in place. First, he had to find a sponsor, a renowned international scientific organization that was sympathetic to the cause. Because scientific research is so expensive, the organization must have a great deal of power and money behind it.* Wake approached several groups before he found what he was looking for.

The International Union for the Conservation of Nature and Natural Resources (IUCN) is composed of more than 500 environmental groups worldwide, including two divisions of the United States government—the U.S. National Park Service and the U.S. Fish and Wildlife Service. IUCN's Species Survival Commission was assigned to work with Wake. Together, with backing from the governments of several countries, including the United States, they set up the Declining Amphibian Populations Task Force (DAPTF) in 1991.

DAPTF's first task was to recruit 1,200 scientists worldwide and ask them to design experiments to answer a single question: Is the simultaneous decline in amphibian populations worldwide just a temporary

---

*Scientists often spend a great deal of time trying to convince private organizations and state and federal agencies to grant them the funds, equipment, and facilities they need to carry out their work.

phenomenon and will the populations rebound, or are amphibians truly disappearing from our planet?

DAPTF offices were set up in thirty countries. The international coordinator was James Vial, professor of wildlife biology at Oregon State University. "We're applying a SWAT team approach to the problem," Vial said at the outset. "We want to get in there, figure out what's going on and get out as fast as possible."[2]

Vial's optimism, while admirable, was ultimately unrealistic, as we shall see.

CHAPTER 3
TRACKING DOWN SUSPECTS

While the DAPTF was getting organized, reports of dead and dying amphibians continued to surface.

- Mount Lassen in California: The Cascades frog used to be found there by the thousands. And now, "We looked at fifty localities, including fifteen where historically the frogs were always found," said biologist Gary Fellers. "We found two. Not frogs in two places. Two frogs total."[1]
- Puerto Rico: A population of up to 3,000 crested toads (*Peltophryne lemur*) faced extinction.
- The southeastern United States: A steep decline had been observed in the populations of the stream-dwelling salamander *Cryptobranchus* and the chorus frog, *Pseudacris triseriata.*
- The southwestern United States: Cynthia Carey's *Bufo boreas* had now disappeared from forty-nine of fifty-nine breeding sites.

Some researchers were estimating that half of all species on Earth might become extinct in the next 30 years. More and more, it looked as though David Wake was right about the "messages" that amphibians were sending us. Are we really heading for some environmental catastrophe? Scientists all over the world wanted to know.

The Cascades frog (*Rana cascadea*) of California is endangered.

One vital goal of the more than 1,200 scientists recruited by DAPTF was to identify causes for any population declines they reported. They were asked to be detectives. The scientists began monitoring amphibian populations and performing experiments to identify the causes of population declines. Once the causes were identified, scientists would at least know what they were up against and could begin to take action.

How Habitat Modification Affects Amphibians

Scientists already agreed on one major cause: the modification—or sometimes outright destruction—of amphibians' habitats by humans. While habitat modification did not explain why Cynthia Carey's Western toads and other amphibians in protected areas were dying, it clearly played a major role in worldwide amphibian decline.

The human population is currently growing at the rate of roughly 90 million people a year. As humans occupy more and more of Earth's land surface, less and less is available for amphibians. As rice paddies in Japan are turned into golf courses, or marshes in California are bulldozed to make way for shopping centers, amphibians and other animals lose their habitats. Herpetologist J. Whitfield Gibbons summed it up this way: "Amphibians don't breed too well in a parking lot."[2]

Habitat modification is a broad term. To better understand it, we need to look at its major components.

Filling In Wetlands

DAPTF researchers determined that 70 percent of Canada's prairie *wetlands*, which had formerly been the home of countless amphibians, were drained and turned into farmland. For a moment, think of those wetlands as houses and apartments in a big city. What do you imagine would become of the human population of that city if 70 percent of those houses and apartments were torn down and never rebuilt?

Clear-Cutting Forests

The world's rain forests are being destroyed at an alarming rate. They once covered between 6 and 7 percent of Earth's land surface. They now cover only about 3 percent. Here are some startling comparisons and statistics.

- At one time, the Amazon rain forest in South America was roughly the size of Western Europe. An area the size of France has already been lost to deforestation, and the destruction continues.
- Between 1981 and 1996, 50 to 75 percent of Guatemala's rain forest was clear-cut or burned.
- A report issued by the Australian Bureau of Statistics states that over half that nation's vegetation has either been significantly disturbed or entirely cleared away, putting more than 1,000 species of native plants and animals in danger of extinction.

When humans cut forests, they are destroying more than trees. Creatures that are not killed as the forests are cut or burned lose their homes and their source of food. This is true for amphibians as well as many other animals. "There's nothing mysterious," said Penn State biologist Blair Hedges. "You cut down trees, and you don't see frogs anymore."[3]

Raising Cattle

Cows are big, clumsy, ravenous animals. They eat everything green in sight. If farmers turn them loose along a stream, they will tear out the plants and break up and flatten the banks. Their grazing may compact the soil so much that it can no longer absorb rainwater. The dry soil that remains is unable to support the abundance of plant life that once made the stream a comfortable home for amphibians and other creatures.

Every year, hundreds of thousands of acres of federally owned wilderness land is leased to cattle ranchers. They turn their cattle loose to graze at will along streams, on hillsides, and in meadows. In the process, they destroy amphibian habitats.

Planting Fish

Following the last ice age, high-elevation lakes in the Sierra Nevada mountains of the western United States became home to frogs—and not fish. Recently, though, people have been stocking these lakes with gamefish that tend to feed on tadpoles. As a result, frog populations in these lakes have declined sharply. In hindsight, David Wake has found that this is one reason for the rapid decline of mountain yellow-legged frogs in California.

Amphibian populations may also be threatened when people release many unwanted pet fish into ponds and lakes. Goldfish, for example, feed on frog eggs. Never release a fish or any other type of pet into the wild.

Tadpoles are a favorite food of rainbow trout like this one.

Direct Causes of Amphibian Deaths

Besides habitat modification, humans upset amphibians' lives in a number of other, more direct, ways. We eat them, use their skins to make wallets and novelty items, keep them as pets, run over them with our cars, and infect them with diseases.

A Feast of Frog Legs

The French alone consume 3,000 to 4,000 tons of frog legs each year. Only the hind legs are used; the rest of the frog is discarded. It takes 20,000 frogs to make 1 ton of frog legs.

Amphibian Knickknacks

In Brazil, the skins of giant toads are sometimes turned into miniature purses. In Thailand, amphibian skins are used to make wallets. A variety of novelty items are also made from amphibians. Imagine an entire orchestra composed of stuffed toads, each toad holding a miniature instrument. This is the sort of thing that consumers can—and do—buy on the open market. As long as people buy such items, amphibians will be killed to produce them.

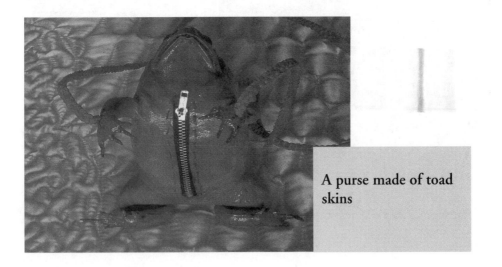

A purse made of toad skins

Amphibians as Exotic Pets

People will also continue to capture amphibians illegally from tropical rain forests and smuggle them out of the country, as long as there are people who want to keep them as pets. Using police dogs, authorities in Lima, Peru, recently discovered 1,000 animals packed in crates bound for California. Among them were several rare species of frogs from Peru's Amazon rain forest. Unfortunately, most of the animals were already dead. An overdose of a sleeping drug administered by their smugglers had poisoned them. It's estimated that the trade in illegal wildlife on the global black market generates $10 billion a year.

Amphibian Roadkill

Frogs and toads like roads because there are no bushes or trees to obstruct their view of flying insects. As a result, automobile traffic running through wetland areas is a constant threat to amphibians. More than 1,000 leopard frogs were killed in just 1 year along a 2-mile (3.2-km) stretch of highway in southern Canada.

The same fate often befalls gopher frogs and striped newts that attempt to cross U.S. Highway 319 near Tallahassee, Florida. A professor at Florida State University is currently using a $40,000 grant to design a tunnel that will give amphibians safe passage underneath the road. Of course, the tunnel will be useless if amphibians cannot be persuaded to use it. To attract the animals, the researcher plans to light the tunnel in a way that mimics starlight.

Making Them Sick

You may wonder how humans can be responsible for amphibian illnesses. When people transport amphibians to different parts of the world—either accidentally or purposely—the animals are exposed to unfamiliar bacteria and viruses. While these *pathogens* pose little or no threat to native creatures, they may be lethal to animals from other parts of the world. Amphibians' permeable skin makes them especially susceptible to diseases they've never encountered before. In addition, gamefish planted in lakes for recreational fishing sometimes carry viruses that turn out to be deadly to amphibians. To make matters worse, scientists know little about the diseases that affect amphibians.

Taking all this into consideration, DAPTF scientists realized they had a lot of hard work in front of them. Like detectives assigned to solve a baffling mystery, these scientists set out in different directions, looking for suspects and chasing down leads. To be effective detectives, they knew that they must be methodical and patient. They realized that most of their leads would go nowhere, but they were determined. They knew they must keep working, relentlessly and methodically, until, through their collective efforts, the suspects were all tracked down.

Ultraviolet Rays as a Suspect

One of these detectives was biology professor Andrew Blaustein, co-chair of the Pacific Northwest Section of DAPTF. The suspect he went after was *ultraviolet (UV) rays* from the sun. Blaustein's research on UV rays began back in 1979. At that time, he and his students were unaware of the worldwide amphibian decline. They were simply conducting a survey of amphibian behavior. What they found was alarming. The eggs of the Cascades frog were perishing in unprecedented numbers, and the researchers couldn't imagine why.

A careful analysis of the ponds and streams where the eggs were laid showed no excess acidity or other signs of pollution. When Blaustein and his students collected fertilized eggs of Cascades frogs and hatched them in the laboratory, the eggs developed normally. The scientists were puzzled. If the eggs thrived in the laboratory, why were they dying in the unpolluted wilderness? Something was wrong out there, but what?

Blaustein recalled laboratory experiments conducted by biologist Robert Worrest in the mid-1970s. Worrest's results suggested that ultraviolet rays—especially UVB rays—could interfere with the development of amphibian *embryos*. These rays, which are known to cause skin cancer in

A male golden
toad (*Bufo periglenes*)
fertilizes eggs as the
female releases them.

The mountain yellow-legged frog (*Rana muscosa*) has been disappearing from its California habitats.

The population of the Cascades frog (*Rana cascadea*) has been declining.

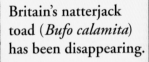

Britain's natterjack toad (*Bufo calamita*) has been disappearing.

The brightly colored harlequin frog (*Atelopus varius*) has vanished from Costa Rica.

The arroyo toad has been disappearing from its southern California habitats.

The appropriately named glass frog of Ecuador

The female Surinam toad carries her eggs on her back until they hatch.

Lush Canadian wetlands like these, which provide homes for countless amphibians, have been drained for farmland.

This section of the Amazon rain forest has been clear-cut for farming.

The crested toad of Puerto Rico (*Peltophryne lemur*) faces extinction.

Automobile traffic in Canada is a life-threatening hazard for leopard frogs like this one.

humans, are also known to suppress the immune system in amphibians.

Blaustein also knew about other studies suggesting that more and more UVB rays were hitting Earth's surface every year. At one time, the rays were repelled by the *ozone* shield. The ozone shield is a layer of air in the stratosphere, 10 to 30 miles (16 to 48 km) up, that wraps around the planet like a protective sheath. By the 1970s, researchers knew that the ozone shield was being seriously eroded by human-made chemicals, such as *chlorofluorocarbons* (CFCs). Although CFCs are now illegal in most parts of the world, they were once widely used to make refrigeration materials, aerosols, and a pesticide called methyl bromide. As CFCs destroyed ozone in the atmosphere, large holes developed in the shield during some parts of the year. Through these holes, UVB rays struck creatures living on the planet. The rays struck their eggs, too.

Unlike chicken eggs, amphibian eggs are not protected by hard shells. Cascade frogs lay their eggs high in the mountains, usually in open shallow water that is exposed to the sun. People who live at high elevations know that they can get a sunburn more quickly than people at sea level. This is because UVB rays are more intense at higher altitudes where the air is thinner. Was exposure to UVB rays preventing the frog eggs from hatching? Blaustein wondered.

This idea made so much sense to Blaustein that he formulated a *hypothesis*—an educated guess—that increasing levels of UVB radiation play a major role in amphibian decline in the wild. Like any good scientist, Blaustein designed an experiment to test his hypothesis. Scientific research often takes a great deal of time and money. Blaustein's study, funded in part by the National Science Foundation and the National Geographic Society, was expected to take 3 years and cost $272,000.

The first phase of Blaustein's experiment focused on how UVB radiation affects *DNA*. All animals have DNA (deoxyribonucleic acid), the molecules that contain instructions for performing the cellular activities necessary for the body to function. Blaustein knew that DNA tends to absorb energy from UVB rays and that this absorbed energy can break down the bonds that hold DNA molecules together. He also knew that when the DNA of an amphibian breaks down, the cells can malfunction. The result may be a total breakdown of the animal's immune system. Remember Cynthia Carey's dead and dying Western toads?

Blaustein also knew that amphibians produce *photolyase*, an *enzyme* that repairs the sort of DNA damage that UVB rays can cause. When Blaustein and his team of researchers measured the levels of photolyase produced by different amphibian species, they found what Blaustein had predicted: Species with low levels of photolyase, such as the Cascades frogs, were in decline; while species with high levels of this protective enzyme, such as the Pacific tree frog (*Hyla regilla*), were doing fine. Pacific tree frogs have three times more photolyase than the endangered Cascades frogs and six times more than Cynthia Carey's endangered Western toads.

Pacific tree frogs, with their high levels of photolyase, could survive—for now at least—while Cascades frogs and Western toads could not. Blaustein and his researchers concluded that their experiment had demonstrated a clear correlation between lack of protection from UVB radiation and declining amphibian populations. While UVB rays were not the sole cause of worldwide amphibian decline, they did appear to be one of the major culprits—or did they?

Did Blaustein's field study, by itself, provide enough evidence to prove a clear correlation between UVB rays and amphibian decline? Correlation is a crucial term in scientific research, and a tricky one. Correlation suggests a cause-effect connection: If A happens, then B results. Blaustein was the first research scientist to precisely measure the effects of UVB in a comparative study in nature. At first glance, the results appeared to be conclusive. But in scientific research, no single experiment necessarily proves a hypothesis.

Blaustein knew he needed more evidence, so he moved into the second phase of his study. The first phase had been conducted within the protective confines of the laboratory; the second phase would be a field study. Field studies involve working with living creatures in the wild. This particular field study was staged in the Cascade Mountains of Oregon at altitudes of 4,000 feet (1,220 m) and higher. There, Blaustein and his researchers collected the freshly laid eggs of Cascades frogs, Western toads, Pacific tree frogs, and Northwestern salamanders. These eggs had a wide range of photolyase levels.

The researchers put the eggs in forty-eight specially designed cages and placed them around lakes and ponds where these frogs, toads, and salamanders normally laid their eggs. They covered some of the cages with clear plastic to filter out UVB rays; others they left unshielded from the sun.

This field study, which was begun in the spring of 1993, should have taken a few months to complete. Instead, it took 2 years. The delay was

Andrew Blaustein tests the effects of UVB rays on frog eggs.

not entirely unexpected for an experiment conducted in the wild. The problems Blaustein and his team ran into included animals not breeding as expected, bad weather, and human vandalism. At one point, someone turned over the cages and destroyed the eggs. Blaustein had to start all over again.

Finally, though, the testing was finished. Would Blaustein find what he expected? His reasoning went this way: If the sun's UVB rays really were destroying amphibian eggs, then species with low levels of photolyase, such as Northwestern salamanders, should do worse than species with high photolyase levels, such as Pacific tree frogs.

And the results? Realistically, scientists can't expect dramatic results from their experiments. They hope to prove their hypotheses, but they know that more often than not, the results are less than conclusive. In some cases, though, the results turn out to be just what they were looking for. In a few cases, the results are truly dramatic. Blaustein's results fell into this last category. Of the unshielded Northwestern salamander eggs—low in photolyase and fully exposed to UVB rays—85.5 percent perished. Of the salamander eggs shielded from UVB rays, only 5 percent perished. The same sort of results were seen with the eggs of Cascades frogs, which also have a low level of photolyase. On the other hand, nearly all the eggs of Pacific tree frogs—high in photolyase—hatched, both shielded and unshielded.

Blaustein and his colleagues decided that their studies had confirmed their hypothesis: Increasing levels of UVB radiation play a major role in amphibian decline in the wild.

A few questions remained, though. What role did *fungus* play in Blaustein's results? The fungus *Saprolegnia* is found naturally in ponds and lakes throughout the Cascades. Like the red leg bacteria that infected Cynthia Carey's toads, *Saprolegnia* can infect amphibian eggs and cause a fatal breakdown in the embryos' power to resist infection. Was it possible that the fungus, and not UVB rays, was responsible for the egg deaths, or did this fungus actually help to confirm Blaustein's hypothesis? Would the

Cascades eggs have survived the fungus infection if they'd been healthier? Did low levels of photolyase combined with the harmful effects of UVB rays make some amphibians too weak to resist infection?

Blaustein had another question: Just how many egg deaths can a population endure before it crashes? And yet another: Does UVB harm tadpoles and adult frogs? Most important of all: Can amphibians adapt to the rapidly increasing level of UVB rays brought about by human activity?

As a species, we humans have been incredibly successful—perhaps too successful for our own good. The consequences of our actions aren't just local anymore; they extend all across Earth's surface and up to 30 miles (48 km) into the atmosphere. No habitat on Earth, no matter how remote it is and no matter how thoroughly we try to protect it, can entirely escape the effects of UVB rays.

Blaustein knew UVB radiation wasn't solely responsible for amphibian declines. For example, it couldn't be the underlying cause of amphibian disappearances in rain forests. After all, the extinct Monteverde golden toad had lived below the dense rain forest canopy in relative safety from the sun's burning rays. Clearly, there were other suspects to be pursued.

CHAPTER 4
THE SEARCH CONTINUES

Global Climate Change

One of the other suspects thought to be behind declining amphibian populations was closely linked with UVB rays and the eroding ozone shield. It was global climate change. Five of the 12 driest months on record and 6 of the 10 warmest years since 1855 occurred during the 1980s. The 1990s have been alarmingly warm too. In fact, 1995 is currently the warmest year in recorded history.

Once again, humans are to blame. For the past 200 years, we have been burning fossil fuels, such as coal, oil, gas, and cutting down and burning forests worldwide. This has brought about a steady increase in the levels of carbon dioxide, methane, and nitrous oxide in the atmosphere. Between 1958 and 1988, the amount of carbon dioxide in the atmosphere increased by 11 percent. Like the windows in a greenhouse, these gases—called greenhouse gases—trap heat from the sun.

When sunlight hits Earth's surface, some of the energy is absorbed and the rest is reflected as *infrared rays.* Greenhouse gases in the atmosphere trap the infrared rays and combine with them to produce energy that heats up the atmosphere. This process is called the *greenhouse effect.*

For Earth's atmosphere to remain healthy, it must be balanced. In other words, the amount of energy going out and the amount of energy coming in must be equal. Our

The greenhouse effect occurs when infrared radiation released from sunlight becomes trapped in Earth's atmosphere instead of released into space.

use of fossil fuels has upset this delicate balance. Scientific studies suggest that the concentration of greenhouse gases in the atmosphere is currently greater than at any other time in Earth's history. Today, the average temperature on Earth's surface is 1°F (0.5°C) greater than it was a century ago. In 1995 alone, the average temperature on Earth rose 0.5°F (0.25°C). Many scientists believe that greenhouse gases are responsible for these increases. They predict that over the next century, average global temperatures will climb another 2 to 6°F (1 to 3°C).

As we burn more and more fossil fuels, the rate of climate change will accelerate. What sorts of global climate changes are scientists predicting?

- Earth will keep heating up due to the greenhouse effect.

- Weather patterns will become less and less predictable and more and more extreme.
- There will be more droughts worldwide, but there also will be more floods.
- Skies will become cloudier, and storms will become more frequent and more extreme. There will be more rain worldwide, because the increase in air temperature leads to an increase in evaporation, which means more precipitation.
- More and more sea ice in the Arctic will melt. In recent scientific expeditions to the far north, researchers have found Arctic ice less than half as thick as expected. In addition, seawater was much less salty than expected because melting ice dilutes the ocean with fresh water. Scientists predict that in years to come the Arctic ice cap may melt entirely in summer. As the total volume of ice decreases, the rate of melting will increase. This is because ice reflects the sun's rays and open ocean water absorbs them. As Arctic ice melts, sea levels will rise worldwide.
- Temperatures will fluctuate more radically and more unpredictably. There will be shifts in the growing season of plants and the active season of animals.
- Worldwide climate conditions will move steadily northward and southward at a rate of 3 to 6 miles (4.8 to 9.6 km) per year. In other words, areas covered by temperate forests today will soon become more tropical.

What does all this mean to amphibians? Although a warmer world would benefit amphibians in some ways, too much of anything can be harmful or even fatal, especially to creatures as dependent on their surroundings as amphibians.

Amphibians are *cold-blooded*. Their body temperature changes with the temperature of their environment. A frog sitting on a warm rock will absorb the rock's heat and warm up; a frog sitting in a cold pond will cool down. On average, amphibians can tolerate temperatures ranging from 28 to 96°F (–2 to 36°C). This tolerance to a wide range of temperatures has enabled amphibians to live in so many different kinds of climates.

But there's a catch. Amphibians can adjust to temporary local changes, but they need overall conditions to remain relatively stable. Their delicate eggs and tadpoles will shrivel and die if ponds, streams, and pools suddenly dry up. Take the golden toads, for instance: In the 2 years immediately preceding their disappearance, rainfall in the Monteverde Cloud Reserve was unusually low. It is likely that many of the golden toads' seasonal breeding ponds dried up early, killing off their young.

How Does Pollution Affect Amphibians?

Unfortunately, scientists don't know exactly how global climate change will affect amphibians or other creatures. They need to collect data over a longer period of time. Scientists face the same obstacle when it comes to another possible cause of amphibian decline—pollution.

When you hear the word *pollution,* you may picture factories dumping toxic waste into rivers; tankers leaking oil into oceans; farmers spraying their crops with pesticides; or cars, trucks, and buses spewing exhaust fumes into the air over cities. The scientists at the 1990 emergency conference at Irvine knew that pollution was getting worse all over the planet, but they had very little data to tell them how it might be affecting amphibians. The data they did have strongly suggested that certain kinds of pollution, such as *acid precipitation* and pesticides, are at least partially responsible for the amphibian population decline.

Like UVB rays, acid rain and snow can affect amphibians in remote places that appear to be free of human activity. They develop when precipitation in the air mixes with pollutants, such as sulfur and nitrate from automobile exhaust and coal-burning factories, to produce sulfuric acid and nitric acid. The results of acid precipitation can be devastating. At least one-fifth of the forests of Europe and vast areas of forest in the northeastern United States and Canada have been hit hard by acid rain.

What does this mean to amphibians? For most species, it's bad news. Acid from acid precipitation accumulates in and around the lakes and ponds where amphibians live. Concentrations of acid are highest in early spring, when large quantities of rain fall and snow melts. Unfortunately, this puts newly laid amphibian eggs at risk. Melting acid snow can be especially deadly by producing an acid pulse—a sudden release of acid into the water—that acts like a dose of poison to amphibian eggs. Studies show that even slightly acidic water can kill the eggs of frogs and toads or result in deformed tadpoles. Salamanders are no better off. Acid precipitation has been blamed for the disappearance of tiger salamanders from parts of the Colorado Rockies.

Some amphibian species actually thrive in water with a high acid content, but they're the exception. The New Jersey Pine Barrens frog is one such species. The water in which these frogs live has a dangerously high acid content. Because the level of acid has remained constant for many years, scientists believe that the frogs have managed to adapt to conditions that would kill other species. Remember, amphibians are highly adaptable creatures, but they need time to adapt to new conditions. Expose them to sudden, human-made changes, such as acid pulses, and they will suffer.

Like acid rain and snow, pesticides can do wide-ranging harm. Every year in the United States, well-meaning farmers, gardeners, and pest-control workers carpet the land with more than 1 billion pounds (454 million kg) of pesticides. Their goal is to control insect pests and produce the kinds of flawless fruits and vegetables that Americans are used to seeing in their supermarkets. Unfortunately, they are harming more than insect pests.

Methoprene is a potent pesticide that short-circuits the growth systems of mosquitoes, biting flies, and fleas so that they never grow into adults capable of reproduction. According to some scientists, methoprene also affects the amphibians that eat the insects. The pesticide appears to interfere with the natural *hormones* that tell an amphibian's body where to grow limbs. The offspring of frogs exposed to large quantities of metho-

Something has interfered with this frog's normal growth patterns, giving it two extra legs.

prene are often missing legs or have extra legs. In some cases, their legs grow out of their chests or from the sides of their heads (see Chapter 5).

Then there's *DDT*, a powerful odorless pesticide that can have horrific long-term effects. DDT remains in the environment long after people have stopped using it. Although it was banned decades ago in the United States and Canada, it is still found in the tissues of many amphibians. When DDT breaks down, it produces chemical substances that interfere with amphibians' reproductive systems, causing some of them to become *sterile*.

When DDT and methoprene were introduced, no one dreamed that they would cause such terrible damage. Similarly, no one knows what damage new chemical pesticides may lead to in the future.

Tragically, amphibians are attracted to the very places where pesticides are most concentrated. When farmers irrigate fields, they also create wetland breeding sites for amphibians. Because pesticides are often spread over these sites to protect the crops, the water and ground may be laced with deadly toxins.

Another Look at the Data

So far we have heard about many different scientists who are extremely concerned about declining amphibian populations. Many of them set out in search of clues that would help them determine what was causing amphibian deaths. It is important to remember, however, that different scientists can look at the same data and come to very different conclusions. Scientists know that their personal biases sometimes influence the way they interpret data. For the most part, they welcome the views of other researchers.

Peter Morin of Rutgers University in New Brunswick, New Jersey, describes amphibian decline as "a phenomenon without much empirical support, not much data." He acknowledges that some herpetologists have found places, such as the Monteverde Cloud Forest, where amphibian populations are dying. But he also thinks that, "Maybe there are places right around the corner that are full of frogs."[1]

In fact, he's right. Frogs continue to thrive in many parts of the world. For example, biologist Blair Hedges, who studies frogs at various sites in the West Indies, has reported that the populations of all twenty-eight species of frogs he's studied have increased in recent years. In addition, two new species have been discovered.

Skeptics like Morin cite two primary reasons for their doubts. One is the data itself, which Morin describes as "not the kind of evidence that a quantitative ecologist would feel comfortable with." He adds, "I'm not saying that people shouldn't study the problem. I'm saying they should do it rigorously and using a protocol [method] that you can apply from one place to the next so that you can compare results."[2]

Herpetologist J. Whitfield Gibbons has doubts about worldwide amphibian decline.

Morin's other primary reason for doubt centers on normal *fluctuations*—natural population changes. Like rodents and insects, amphibians have always been subject to large population swings. Herpetologist J. Whitfield Gibbons of the University of Georgia has been surveying amphibian populations for more than two decades. He says that his most dramatic finding has been how variable the amphibian community is naturally. He notes that while amphibians have disappeared from protected habitats in Ecuador and Venezuela, these very same species are thriving in nearly identical habitats in Colombia. Peter Morin adds that more real data on populations are needed. Analysis of rigorously collected data is the only way to know for sure whether amphibian populations are really steadily decreasing, or simply fluctuating naturally. It is very possible that current population decreases will soon end, and populations will begin growing again.

The sort of long-term amphibian studies that Morin calls for are rare. One of the few, and one of the most complete, is a census study conducted over a 12-year period (1978 to 1990) at Rainbow Bay, South Carolina—a remote, protected amphibian breeding pond. The researchers, under the

AMPHIBIANS' UPS AND DOWNS

It is characteristic of amphibian populations to rise and fall dramatically. One scientist surveyed population swings of cane toads (*Bufo marinus*) at four ponds on a farm on the Caribbean island of Trinidad. The results are shown in the table below.

Cane Toads at Haven Hill Farm, Trinidad		
Year	Calling Days*	Males Seen**
1987	131	222
1988	164	308
1989	128	208
1990	91	143
1991	84	147
1992	65	112
1993	40	74
1994	62	113
1995	32	76
1996	102	222
1997	102	213

* Number of days in that year when the toads were heard calling. (Male toads do nearly all the calling, mainly to attract females.)

** Number of days in that year when male cane toads were spotted along the edges of ponds.

This survey was conducted by Victor C. Quesnel and published in DAPTF's *Froglog* newsletter Number 27 (see the Online Sites section at the back of the book). Notice how this particular amphibian population rose, then fell, then rose again during an 11-year period.

direction of Joseph H. K. Pechmann, sectioned off the pond with fences and traps. Working in one fenced-off section at a time, researchers caught and identified the amphibians living there, then released them into another section of the pond. In this way they could document exactly how many and what kinds of amphibians were living in the pond from month to month and year to year.

In published reports on his study, Pechmann urges caution. Amphibian populations have always been known to rise and fall more rapidly and extremely than other animal populations. If you look at certain portions of his data taken over a given week or month, he notes, you would spot steep declines that you might at first blame on human causes. But if you look at these steep declines in the context of all the data over all the years, you'd be just as likely to see them as natural population fluctuations. "It remains an open question," Pechmann writes, "whether declines and disappearances of some frog species in isolated, pristine environments represent a natural fluctuation or some subtle effect of human activities that we don't understand. My money is on the natural fluctuations, but I can't prove that. Only further research will say for sure."[3]

So, we can add natural population fluctuations to the list that includes pollution, global climate change, UVB rays, and habitat modification. All are potential causes of worldwide amphibian decline. They are all pieces in a giant puzzle.

Fitting the Pieces Together

One person who is trying to take all of these puzzle pieces into consideration is DAPTF scientist Cynthia Carey. Ever since her encounter with the dead and dying *Bufo boreas* in 1973, Carey has been wondering what could have caused the immune systems of so many toads to collapse. In 1992 she began a long-term study, funded with a National Science Foundation grant, to test her own hypothesis: She believes that worldwide amphibian decline is due to a complex combination of causes that, taken together, result in the breakdown of amphibian immune systems.

Before Carey could do this, she had to learn more about the immune systems of amphibians. Amphibians have been studied very little in comparison with other animals. Most ecologists have ignored amphibians in favor of birds and mammals. As a result, Carey began her research project by conducting an intensive examination of a healthy toad's immune system. She wanted to know how it works and what might cause it to fail.

When Carey completes this step of her project, she intends to find out what happens when healthy toads are exposed to stress factors such as acid water, UVB rays, and pesticides. Amphibians' behavior is controlled by hormones, and hormone output increases when amphibians are subjected to higher than normal levels of stress. Frogs will not reproduce under these stress levels and are much more susceptible to disease. Acting together, these stress factors may be responsible for the breakdown of amphibians' delicate immune systems.

The majority of scientists working to solve this mystery agree that a variety of causes appear to be responsible. DAPTF scientist David Wake said, "I don't see a single virus. My theory is that it's general *environmental degradation.* That's the worst thing. Frogs are telling us about the environment's overall health. They are the medium and the message."[4] Another message came a few years later. As DAPTF scientists all over the world were busy looking for clues to the cause of amphibian decline, a new mystery unfolded and a new alarm was sounded.

CHAPTER 5
NIGHTMARE AT NEY'S POND

It was August 8, 1995. Eight middle school and high school students from New Country School in Le Sueur, Minnesota, set out on a field trip. New Country School is a year-round charter school—a public school with an alternative curriculum—dedicated to hands-on learning in the community. The students weren't planning to make any earthshaking discoveries on their trip. They just wanted to observe the plants and animals in and around a local pond. The pond they chose was located on Don Ney's farm near the town of Henderson, which is 55 miles (88 km) southwest of Minneapolis. They were prepared to look, listen, and write down their observations in field notebooks. The students had no idea that their perfectly ordinary field trip was about to turn into a nightmare.

The teacher leading the group was Cindy Reinitz. Not long after arriving at the pond, 13-year-old Jeff Fish came to Reinitz with a northern leopard frog—one of many in and around the pond. But this frog was different; something was wrong with its leg. Jeff was very upset. He thought he might have accidentally stepped on the frog. Why did it look so strange?

Soon, other students came to their teacher with more odd-looking frogs. Student Elaine Farley remembers: "I thought I broke its leg because it was sticking straight out. And someone else caught a frog, and they go, 'you broke

Teacher Cindy Reinitz works with students near Ney's Pond in Minnesota.

its leg too. . . .' So we just started catching more frogs, and they all had broken legs, we thought."[1] There were hundreds of frogs with unusual legs. Some frogs had too many legs, and others did not have enough legs. Still others had legs that were twisted and misshapen or that split at the knee and branched off into two or more different feet.

At first, it looked as though only the frogs' legs were unusual. Eventually, though, the students started noticing problems with the frogs' eyes: missing eyes, extra eyes, eyes protruding from backs and shoulders. It was bizarre, Reinitz remembers.

Despite their excitement and horror, this teacher and her students didn't forget why they'd come to Ney's pond. They took out their notebooks and carefully recorded their observations. They also took photographs of deformed frogs using a digital camera. This would allow them to post the photos on the school's Web site. (See the Online Sites section at the back of this book.)

When the group returned to the school, Cindy Reinitz made some urgent phone calls. What happened next amazed everyone. First, a local newspaper ran a story about the deformed frogs at Don Ney's pond. Then, 10 days later, a TV station featured the story on the evening news. A week after that, on August 25, the Associated Press, a news agency that supplies stories to newspapers and radio and TV stations nationwide, sent out a story on the nightmare at Ney's pond.

The school was immediately flooded with phone calls from all around the United States. The media blitz had begun. Reinitz and her students spent the rest of that day out at the pond telling their story to TV reporters. Two stations actually brought satellite trucks to the scene to do live, on-the-spot reports. That was just the beginning. A full year later, calls about the deformed frogs were still coming in to the school on a daily basis.

One of Reinitz's phone calls had been to Judy Helgen, a research scientist at the Minnesota Pollution Control Authority (MPCA). At first, Helgen considered the deformities to be a strictly local problem. After all, the pond was located in an agricultural area. It seemed likely that residue from pesticides used by local farmers had poisoned the pond, triggering the deformities.

As it turned out, however, Ney's pond was not the only place where deformed amphibians were showing up in alarming numbers. Helgen began getting calls from all over the state. By the summer of 1996, more than 175 reports of deformed frogs had come in from 54 of Minnesota's 87 counties, as well as from a dozen other states and even some other countries.

The Search for an Answer

No one could explain the deformities. Scientists looked at the available information and began to develop hypotheses. It didn't take long for several different schools of thought to spring up. Some thought that the whole thing—hundreds of deformed frogs in one little pond—must be either a deliberate hoax or the result of someone carelessly dumping something highly toxic like paint thinner into the pond.

Others, including Martin Ouellet, blamed pesticides. Ouellet worked for the Canadian Wildlife Service. He had documented deformities in frogs from agricultural areas in Canada. A biologist in Great Britain reported a striking similarity between the deformed Minnesota frogs and frogs he'd been working with in his London laboratory. The frogs had grown extra limbs when they were exposed to retinoic acid, a human-made chemical. Similar chemicals are produced when the pesticide methoprene breaks down in the environment.

Stanley K. Sessions, a developmental biologist at Hartwick College in Oneonta, New York, disagreed with the pesticide hypothesis. He blamed the deformities on *parasites*, organisms that live off other organisms. He had noticed that the hind limbs and limb buds of many of the amphibians he studied were infected with *trematodes*. During the first stage of this microscopic parasitic flatworm's complex life cycle, the eggs are found inside snakes. When the eggs leave a snake's body in its feces, they are consumed by pond snails. Inside the snails, the trematode eggs develop into hundreds of thousands of swimming *larvae*. Eventually, the larvae leave the snail in search of yet another *host*.

The trematode larvae's hosts of choice are tadpoles. "They're sitting there in the mud searching for a host," Sessions says, "and if an unfortunate tadpole happens to land there, they home in on it, punch a hole into its skin, and squeeze in. This takes only about 30 seconds. I've seen it under a microscope."[2] They tend to burrow in around the limbs and limb buds, using potent digestive enzymes and sharp little spearlike probes. To envision the process, says Sessions, imagine someone slowly pushing pencils into your body. Once the trematodes are underneath the tadpole's skin, they split the limb bud apart. This can cause a tadpole to grow extra limbs.

According to Sessions's hypothesis, frog deformities are caused by trematodes. He believed that the presence of trematodes around the hind

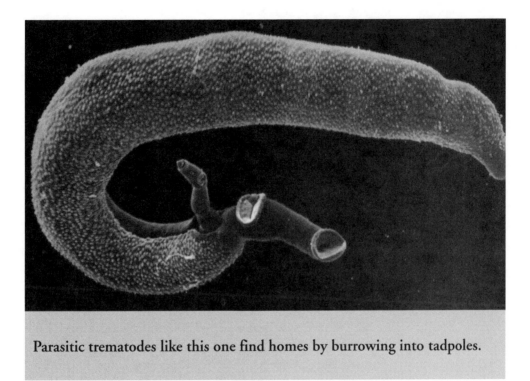

Parasitic trematodes like this one find homes by burrowing into tadpoles.

limbs and limb buds of developing amphibians upsets the animals' normal growth processes. Sessions tested his idea with what he called "the bead experiment." He implanted tiny plastic beads the size of trematodes into the developing limb buds of tadpoles and raised them in the laboratory.

Several of the tadpoles in which the plastic beads were implanted eventually developed extra limbs. Based on this evidence, Sessions concluded that trematodes cause amphibians to produce extra limbs. He claimed that amphibians with missing limbs are the victims of predators. When asked about the Minnesota frog deformities, Sessions said, "I will not be surprised at all if it turns out this has been an enormous Chicken Little thing."[3] In other words, a false alarm.

Kathy Converse of the National Wildlife Health Center in Madison, Wisconsin, had another idea. She had studied seventy of the deformed Minnesota frogs, along with normal frogs. In a microscopic analysis of their tissues, she'd seen parasites of the kind Sessions was working with in both normal and deformed frogs. Why, she asked, did only some of the infected frogs develop deformities? She also pointed out that Sessions had not used frogs native to Minnesota in his bead experiment. In fact, he had never even personally examined any of the deformed Minnesota frogs.

David Hoppe, a herpetologist at the University of Minnesota, sided with Converse. He had a valid question of his own. He knew that trematodes had been around for millions of years, so he wondered why no one had ever noticed this number of deformities before. Hoppe had studied amphibians for decades. From 1975 to 1995, he'd observed and handled thousands of Minnesota frogs. In all those years, he'd seen only two frogs with limb deformities. Yet in 1996 alone, he saw more than 200 deformed frogs. Like Ouellet, Hoppe thought pesticides might be to blame.

Hoppe worked with Robert McKinnell, a biologist who had spent even longer studying frogs—40 years. In all those years, McKinnell had never seen abnormalities like these. In McKinnell's experience, deformities show up in only 1 in 10,000 frogs. He was concerned, very concerned. "Sometimes I wake up in the middle of the night and I say, 'Good grief, what is this?'"[4]

Hillary Carpenter, a scientist at the Minnesota Department of Health, also suspected that human-made contaminants in the water might be the cause of the deformities. But she went a step beyond concern for endangered amphibians when she said, "What's driving this whole issue is . . . the potential for effects on human health."[5] Like some other researchers, she thought amphibians might be acting like a canary in a coal mine.

Meanwhile, the professionals weren't the only ones working to solve the mystery of Minnesota's deformed frogs. Cindy Reinitz and her stu-

Professor Robert McKinnell is concerned about the sudden increase in frog deformities.

dents came up with a plan. They decided to make more trips to Ney's pond to look for clues. They interviewed reporters, cameramen, and engineers. They wrote articles for newsletters and magazines, and they maintained their Web site, answering e-mail from all over the United States. Even if they didn't find any answers, they would learn valuable lessons along the way.

"I learned how to ask the right questions to problems I needed answers to," wrote ninth-grader Betsy Kroon.[6] Tenth-grader Ryan Fisher learned to look at things like a scientist and a detective combined: "Instead of focusing on the obvious, I had to take the initiative to notice the details that might be overlooked." He also learned that "you can make a difference in your town, your city, or even your country."[7] Reinitz's students testified before the Minnesota legislature in favor of a bill to help fund deformed frog research. They also won awards—including one for $12,500, which the school used to buy science equipment.

What did Reinitz think of her students after all this? "When all our health officials and corporate CEOs are as alert, insightful, and concerned as those children, we'll no longer have to rely on frogs to give us warning."[8]

A Frightening Announcement

While Cindy Reinitz and her students were hard at work, the controversy over what was causing frog deformities kept heating up—month after month, year after year. A major flashpoint came on September 30, 1997. Peder Larson, commissioner of the MPCA, told the reporters at a St. Paul press conference that scientists had found something wrong with water samples taken from what they termed "hot spots" near two wetland sites where deformed frogs had been found.

Biologists from the National Institute of Environmental Health Sciences (NIEHS) had raised some frog embryos in these "hot-spot" samples, including water taken directly from the kitchen taps of families living in these areas. At the same time, they had raised other frog embryos in "normal" water. The results seemed conclusive—and alarming. They found that 75 percent of the embryos raised in "hot-spot" water had deformities, while none of the embryos raised in "normal" water were deformed.

Public officials know they must be careful when releasing potentially alarming public-health information. The findings of the NIEHS study could upset a lot of people, maybe even cause a panic. When Peder Larson made the announcement, he said, "These findings give us a big piece of the puzzle we've been looking for in regard to the problems with the frogs. It does not provide evidence of a human health link, but it does underline the need to look more closely at what all this may mean for the environment. If the frog investigation was a priority for us before, it's even more so now."[9]

Dr. James Burkhart of the NIEHS added that although the findings did show a correlation between groundwater and frog deformities, researchers did not yet know exactly why the water was causing the deformities. He said that they wouldn't know until more data were collected.

Another official at the press conference, Dr. George Lucier of the NIEHS, confirmed that there was something in the groundwater—something extraordinarily potent—causing the frog deformities. It could be human-made contaminants or some natural agent, such as pond plants or algae. He assured everyone that scientists from the NIEHS, the National

Wildlife Health Center, and the U.S. Environmental Protection Agency (EPA) were busy subjecting groundwater samples to additional tests. They hoped to find what was causing the deformities. According to Mark Gernes of the MPCA, scientists were, in essence, trying to pull the water apart, as you would take apart a watch to see what made it tick. He estimated that test results would be available in about 2 months. In the meantime, Larson announced, the state would provide free bottled water to the families whose kitchen taps had produced "hot-spot" water.

Despite efforts to avoid controversy, the press conference succeeded only in stirring it up. Andrew Blaustein stated that, in his opinion, the press conference was alarmist and premature. Providing bottled drinking water made it seem as though the problem was very serious. It implied that the groundwater might be hazardous to human health. In reality, tests had shown that while the water might be unsafe for amphibians, it was perfectly safe for human consumption. Joe Tietge, a research biologist with the EPA, put it this way: "Anybody with a tropical fish aquarium knows that if you fill it with tap water it will kill the fish. That doesn't mean your tap water isn't safe to drink."[10]

The scientists who conduct experiments related to public health must also exercise caution. Any potentially alarming conclusions they might draw from their test results had better be firmly grounded by experiments conducted under exactly the right conditions—no mistakes.

In this case, the groundwater experiments had been conducted by NIEHS scientists who, according to EPA scientists, had committed a fundamental technical mistake. Instead of using embryos of frogs native to Minnesota, the NIEHS scientists had used embryos of the African clawed frog, a non-native frog often used in laboratory tests. In doing this, they had failed to take into account the fact that African clawed frog embryos need water that contains certain salts—salts not present in the Minnesota groundwater—to grow normally.

When scientists from the EPA's Mid-Continent Ecology Lab in Duluth duplicated the NIEHS experiments using water with the proper

Mark Gernes of the Minnesota Pollution Control Agency examines a deformed frog.

ratio of salts, their results showed no deformities at all. The African clawed frog embryos developed perfectly normally.

Yes, the NIEHS now agreed, they should have added these salts. They repeated their original experiments with the proper ratio of salts. Surprisingly, their results did not match those of the EPA. The NIEHS researchers got the same results they got the first time. The frog embryos developed abnormally.

What was going on? Two groups of highly competent scientists had performed the same experiment using the same components under the same conditions and had come up with very different results. No wonder this issue was clouded in controversy and confusion.

The Controversy Heats Up

It wasn't long before the confusion got worse. Gil Veith, an EPA official, accused the NIEHS of issuing their flawed test results prematurely in order to make newspaper headlines. He insisted that NIEHS scientists weren't experienced with amphibian species, but that the scientists at the EPA Duluth laboratory were. He reiterated that the EPA's results clearly showed that there was nothing in any of the Minnesota groundwater samples that could be harmful to amphibians or to humans.

Dr. James Burkhart of the NIEHS responded by blaming the MPCA. He said that the NIEHS had originally had no intention of making the test results public until they had subjected them to further analysis. He claimed that the MPCA had insisted that the NIEHS release their findings. The NIEHS had done so, but against their better judgment.

Judy Helgen, who managed the MPCA side of the project, responded by defending her agency. The MPCA didn't want to make the test results public either, she said. As scientists, they were accustomed to doing their work in private, and they thought they were already doing too much of it in the public eye. The last thing the MPCA wanted was more publicity. But the news of the bottled water was starting to leak out to the media, she said, and MPCA officials feared these news leaks might lead to a pub-

Judy Helgen (right) of the Minnesota Pollution Control Agency helped conduct groundwater tests in areas where deformed frogs were found.

lic panic. That was why they'd insisted on releasing the NIEHS test results—to reassure the public that there was nothing to worry about.

Another side of the groundwater story surfaced in March 1998, when MPCA officials reluctantly released results of their own tests of groundwater in the "hot-spot" areas. This time they had tested drinking water from thirty-eight different wells, and the results were baffling. Samples from five of the wells produced large numbers of deformities in newly fertilized frog eggs—but not a single one of these five "hot-spot" wells had produced deformities during the first round of testing. Even stranger, none of the eggs from wells that had originally been designated "hot spots" were growing into deformed frogs. In other words, the water that appeared to be safe during the original testing period appeared to be dangerous now, and the water that appeared to be dangerous during the original testing period appeared to be safe now.

These results confused everyone. As to the state-supplied water issue, the MPCA decided that since everything was still so uncertain, the families that had been receiving bottled water would continue to receive it. But, they restated, that didn't mean there was anything to be concerned about. The NIEHS agreed with the MPCA. As confusing as the results were, said NIEHS project leader James Burkhart, there was no cause for alarm. The tests had not provided any conclusive evidence of danger to human health.

Why, then, was the state still providing bottled water to the families whose well water had now been found to be perfectly safe? Controversy, conflict, confusion—it was hard to find much in the way of consensus among the scientists from the various agencies involved. They did agree on one thing, though: Instead of a single cause, a complex combination of causes was at work. Tracking them down would surely be, in the words of David Wake, "a scientific nightmare."[11]

CHAPTER 6
THE MYSTERY DEEPENS

The results of the next significant study on amphibian decline were published in 1996 by Charles Drost and Gary Fellers of the U.S. Geological Survey in California. Drost and Fellers approached the problem from a unique historical perspective.

Between 1915 and 1919, scientists Tracy Storer and Joseph Grinnell had conducted a detailed biological survey of the back country in Yosemite National Park in eastern California. During those 4 years, they managed to explore and describe seventy different amphibian breeding sites. Seventy-five years later, after reading Storer and Grinnell's results, Drost and Fellers decided to follow in their footsteps. They planned to re-survey the same amphibian breeding sites and compare their results with those collected 75 years earlier. Nothing quite like this had ever been done before. Drost and Fellers's report was the first detailed look at how an amphibian community changed over such an extended period of time.

Drost and Fellers's results revealed a startling population crash. Three of the seven species of frogs and toads that Storer and Grinnell described had disappeared entirely from the breeding sites; the other four native species were in significant decline. The scientists found only a single *Bufo boreas* (Cynthia Carey's Western toad). Seventy-five years earlier, Storer and Grinnell had described *Bufo boreas*

Biologist Gary Fellers sees danger for amphibians all across the United States.

as exceedingly abundant. Ronald Heyer, a herpetologist and chair of the global Declining Amphibian Populations Task Force, called the report "chilling." Based on their results, Drost and Fellers estimated that one-third of the frogs and toads in the United States seemed to be in imminent danger.

Not everyone agreed with this conclusion. J. Whitfield Gibbons, a herpetologist who worked on the 12-year Rainbow Bay study (see Chapter 4), said that what he'd learned from the census was that amphibian populations fluctuate naturally. He believed it was normal for there to be many amphibians at a given site one year and few the next, or vice-versa. According to Gibbons, Drost and Fellers's findings didn't prove that amphibians were dying off due to some catastrophic set of circumstances. They just showed how nature works.

When Fellers heard Gibbons's interpretation of the data, he said, "The naysayers can always say you won't know if you're seeing a trend until you survey these animals for a hundred years. But if you go to Yosemite and visit every pond, lake, and stream that is suitable for frogs and find major declines—or absolutely nothing—where there once was abundance, that's well beyond the scope of a natural fluctuation."[1]

One question remained. If the amphibian declines at Yosemite were not the result of natural population fluctuations, why were they happening?

Drost and Fellers discounted habitat destruction. The Yosemite back country has been protected under the National Park system for all of the 75 years between the two censuses. The land was virtually undisturbed. The scientists also discounted drought because dry conditions were as common 75 years ago as they are today. They also decided that fish-planting was not responsible because the areas around the lakes and ponds where fish had been planted were not among the areas showing significant amphibian declines.

One possibility was chemical contamination. Pesticides might be drifting into the park from distant farmlands. As they tried to identify the reason for declining populations, they had to consider the thriving population of *Rana catesbeiana*, a bullfrog that had not been mentioned at all in the original census. In fact, there were no bullfrogs at all in California until the late 1800s. People introduced them into the area to provide frog legs for restaurants. Bigger and heartier than the native species, *Rana catesbeiana* are known to consume other, smaller frogs as a substantial part of their diet. Thus, bullfrogs were a second possible cause of amphibian decline in Yosemite.

Andrew Blaustein believes that ultraviolet rays from the sun are a chief cause of amphibian decline.

Pacific treefrogs (*Hyla regilla*) have high levels of an enzyme that protects them from ultraviolet rays.

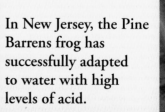

In New Jersey, the Pine Barrens frog has successfully adapted to water with high levels of acid.

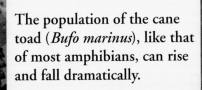

The population of the cane toad (*Bufo marinus*), like that of most amphibians, can rise and fall dramatically.

The endangered cave salamander (*Eurycea lucitga*)

The word salamander comes from an ancient Greek word meaning "fire animal."

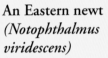

An Eastern newt
(*Notophthalmus viridescens*)

A spotted salamander
(*Ambystoma maculatum*)

The three-striped poison dart frog *(Epipedobattes trivittatus)* produces poison from skin glands to protect itself from predators.

Dr. Scott McRobert of the St. Joseph's University biodiversity lab runs an experiment with poison dart frogs.

The brightly colored blue dart frog, *Dendrobates azureus*

Another brightly-colored poison dart frog, *Dendrobates imitator*

The Wyoming toad
has been saved from
extinction.

GOLD NUGGETS AND FROGS LEGS

In the mid-1800s, President James K. Polk announced that gold had been found in northern California. Before that time, no more than 10,000 people lived in the entire state, and most of those in the southern part. Two-thirds of the hundreds of thousands who flocked to northern California seeking gold were born in other countries, mostly in Europe.

These new arrivals were accustomed to European cooking, and they were fond of eating meals out. As a result, restaurant owners in and around San Francisco began bringing over thousands of chefs from France to satisfy the ever-growing demand for French restaurant food, such as frog legs.

In 1885, some 118,000 frogs were taken from the marshes of California's Central Valley. Americans' appetite for frog legs didn't end with the California Gold Rush. Between 1981 and 1984, 6.5 million tons of frog meat was imported into the United States each year. Those 6.5 million tons were made up entirely of legs, the only part of the frog that is consumed.

Many people around the world find frog legs, like those at the bottom left, good to eat.

More Amphibian Declines Reported

In the end, Drost and Fellers's historical survey sounded more alarms, but yielded no conclusive answers. It had only deepened the ominous mystery of amphibian decline. Meanwhile, the decline continued all around the world.

- In Australia, a 1996 government report declared that the nation's environment was under dire threat from human activities—activities vital to the nation's economy. Wildlife was threatened by mining and agricultural activities. Half of the nation's vegetation had been either significantly disturbed or cleared away altogether for farmland, and farmers were using 70 percent of the nation's water supply. As a result, the report declared, Australia had more endangered amphibians than any other nation on Earth.
- In industrial regions of the Ukraine in eastern Europe, DAPTF investigations showed that the natural chemical composition of water in aquatic ecosystems was changing, due primarily to chemical pollution. As a result, amphibian populations were declining.
- In the mountainous tea-growing regions of Sri Lanka, frog species that were once abundant had virtually disappeared. Scientists suspected that decreases in the populations of *Polypedates eques* and *Rana greeni* were the result of pesticides used by tea-growers.
- Recent surveys of Costa Rica's Monteverde region, former home of the golden toad and harlequin frog, have shown a steady decline of twenty different amphibian species. By 1998, half of Costa Rica's frog population had vanished. Some of the blame may lie with long stretches of drier-than-normal weather, but scientists can't be sure.

The list goes on. There are many declining amphibian populations and many possible causes, but no definitive answers. Reports of deformities also continue to escalate.

In October 1996, Richard Levey, an aquatic biologist with the Vermont Agency for Natural Resources, surveyed Lake Champlain in Vermont. He and another researcher collected 230 leopard frogs from 4 different sites on the eastern shore, and found that 16 percent were deformed.

In 1997, the North American Reporting Center for Amphibian Malformations (NARCAM) was set up in Raleigh-Durham, North Carolina, to serve as a national clearinghouse for these data. Deformed amphibian sightings could be reported through a Web site or a toll-free number (see the How You Can Help section at the back of the book). Minnesota led the nation with confirmed reports from some 200 sites across the state. Meanwhile, the search for answers also continued—as did the controversy.

The Research Continues

Andrew Blaustein continued his research on the effects of UVB rays on amphibians (see Chapter 3). Now he was using the eggs of long-toothed salamanders for his field tests in Oregon lakes. He exposed some of the eggs to unfiltered sunlight and others to sunlight from which UVB rays had been filtered out. Then he compared the results. Eighty-five percent of the embryos from eggs exposed to unfiltered sunlight died. Of the 15 percent that did hatch, all but 4 of the animals were deformed. In contrast, 98 percent of the eggs shielded from UVB rays hatched. Nearly all the resulting animals were normal.

Blaustein insisted that this was proof that excess UVB radiation in nature can cause death and deformity in amphibian species. Dennis B. Fenn of the U.S. Geological Survey agreed, adding that we had better start taking the effects of UVB seriously.

But EPA scientist Gary Ankley, while agreeing that Blaustein's study is "a serious thing," said that "it would be simplistic to blame all of the declines on one factor at this time."[2]

Ankley is not alone. Many researchers continue to believe that many factors, taken together, are responsible. DAPTF scientist Cynthia Carey is one of them. As part of her continuing study of various stress factors on amphibians' nervous systems, she too has been testing the effects of UVB rays. She insists that while UVB exposure may be a contributing factor to the overall stress responsible for the breakdown of amphibian immune systems, it is not the sole cause. Her recent research shows that other possible causes include exposure to high levels of metals and acids or to long periods of cold temperatures.

And what about pesticides? The methoprene issue is still very much alive (see Chapter 4). In September 1997, research scientists in California issued test results suggesting that the blame for the Minnesota frog deformities might lie with this widely used pesticide. One of these scientists, Bruce Blumberg, a professor at the Salk Institute in San Diego, advised that we should look very carefully at methoprene and determine its effects on amphibians.

Wallmark International, the makers of methoprene, issued statements criticizing Blumberg and his fellow researchers for using concentrations of methoprene higher than the recommended dosage in their experiments. Blumberg promptly countered, "The levels we use are actually much lower than the levels you encounter when you set off a flea bomb in your house or when you take your dog or your cat to be flea-dipped."[3] Then the EPA's Joe Tietge joined the controversy—on Wallmark's side. The EPA had performed their own experiments, he announced, and had ruled out methoprene as a cause of frog deformities.

A Brand-New Idea

Around this same time, an American biologist doing field research in Costa Rica came up with an entirely new angle on amphibian decline. Karen Lips of Southern Illinois University in Carbondale, Illinois, formulated what she called the extinction wave hypothesis. Here's how this hypothesis came about. Lips had been studying stream-breeding frogs at the Zona Protectorada Las Tablas in the mountains of Costa Rica's Puntarena Province since 1990. This site is part of the Amistad Biosphere Reserve.

Beginning in 1992, Lips observed frogs dying off in alarming numbers at this protected site. By 1996, five frog species populations were reduced by 90 percent. Lips could find no direct cause for this mysterious decline, but something indirect did strike her. This site was south of the Monteverde Cloud Reserve where, in 1988, the famous golden toad had disappeared, followed by the harlequin frog. Could it be that a disease of some kind, a deadly *epidemic*, was moving southward through Central America?

Lips set to work testing her hypothesis. If the epidemic was moving southward, then she too must move in that direction. Lips visited the Reserva Forestal Fortuna in Chirique Province, Panama, which she had surveyed 3 years earlier. During that earlier survey of seven streams, Lips had found fifty-five species of amphibians. During this new survey, 3 years later, Lips could find only twenty-four species, and all of these were along only two of the seven streams. The other five streams, which had been abundant with frogs only 3 years earlier, had virtually no healthy frogs now.

There were unhealthy frogs, though. Lips discovered fifty-four dead or dying frogs along these five streams. Many of the dead frogs still looked as if they were alive, some sitting in perched positions, as if about to jump. Many of the dying frogs were lethargic, unable to gather their legs up to sit. Others were having convulsions; their limbs and heads were trembling. Lips also found a tadpole with a bloody lesion. These symptoms were similar to those recently reported at an Australian site. Researchers had discovered that the frogs at that site were infected with a virus.

Putting the Fortuna survey information together with what she knew of Monteverde and Las Tablas, Lips concluded that all three sites, which had similar climates and plant and animal life, had all suffered similar declines of amphibians. She believed that these declines were all caused by the same agent. What was this agent? Lips couldn't be sure, but she believed that "the directional movement suggests a 'front' or wave of mortality . . . a pattern more typical of disease epidemics" than habitat destruction or climate change.[4]

Like so many other potential causes advanced by scientists for worldwide amphibian decline, Lips's extinction-wave hypothesis will remain just that—an educated guess—until research scientists in other countries perform similar experiments that yield similar results. Lips sent fifty of the Fortuna casualties back to the United States for tissue analysis. The results showed that the frogs may have been killed by a newly discovered fungus.

In June 1998, a group of scientists reported that another newly discovered fungus had killed a total of 120 frogs and toads belonging to 19 species in Australia and Panama. The same fungus also struck six species of amphibians in U.S. zoos and aquariums. The scientists weren't sure exactly how the fungus killed the frogs. They advanced two possibilities: The fungus may exude a lethal toxin that poisons the frogs, or it may suffocate them by coating their undersides and legs, thus keeping their permeable skin from breathing. According to an article about the discovery in *New Scientist*, a British science magazine, "The scientists don't yet know if the fungus is the primary cause of death, or is killing animals weakened by other factors, such as ultraviolet radiation penetrating the atmosphere due to the thinned ozone layer or agricultural chemicals."[5]

Despite almost two decades of research, by 1998 there were still no clear answers. There were plenty of suspects and plenty of intriguing possibilities, but little in the way of proof. In 1992, James Vial, DAPTF coordinator, had said, "We're applying a SWAT team approach to the problem. We want to get in there, figure out what's going on, and get out as fast as possible."[6] In the years since Vial first uttered those optimistic words, the mystery has only deepened.

CONCLUSION
THE WARNINGS CONTINUE

The continuing mystery of worldwide amphibian decline will not be solved until scientists have more data. But data come from research, and research is expensive—especially field studies. No matter how much dedicated work scientists devote to solving this global problem, they can't do much meaningful work without funding. Unfortunately, most funding for scientific research comes from government agencies, where amphibian decline has never been high on the list of priorities.

There are signs that this attitude is changing, though. In May 1998, in the offices of the U.S. Department of the Interior, high government officials and influential scientists gathered at the request of the National Science Foundation. Among them was Bruce Babbitt, secretary of the interior. Also in attendance were David Wake of DAPTF, and the heads of the Environmental Protection Agency and National Science Foundation. The subject of the meeting was declining amphibian populations. The conclusions that these scientists and government officials came to nicely summarize the current state of this issue.

1. Worldwide amphibian decline is a reality. "For the first time, I think we have a major group of organisms—a group of vertebrates that's experiencing a substantial number of extinctions over a short peri-

od of time," said David Wake. According to Bruce Babbitt, "We have enough information coming in now to know unequivocally and without question that there is a worldwide decline; that extinctions are taking place; that the deformities that we are seeing in these amphibians, particularly frogs, are not a natural back ground level; that something is happening out there."[1]

2. Amphibians are disappearing in and around cities and on farmland where human activities have modified, and in some cases destroyed, amphibian habitats. Amphibians are also dying in completely unexpected places—remote areas that have been protected for decades. Examples include Cynthia Carey's Western toads in the Colorado wilderness, the golden toads in the Monteverde Cloud Reserve, and the gastric brooder frogs in the mountains of Australia.

3. We still do not have a complete picture of why amphibians are dying. Possible causes include erosion of the ozone shield, global climate change, acid precipitation, parasites, pesticides, and an epidemic of deadly viruses. Scientists are certain of this much, though: The causes are closely connected to human activities. As Babbitt says, "There's clearly some external cause that's probably related to something that we are doing across the broader landscape."[2]

4. No single factor is responsible for the decline. It is the result of many causes that are all working together. These multiple causes, this interactive complex of "insults to the environment," are signs that we are living on a planet that, year by year, is coming under greater and greater stress. As David Wake says, "If it's habitat destruction, there's something we can do about it. We can build fences or we can stop people from going into places. But if it's generalized stress and generalized environmental degradation, then I'm afraid that we are the cause and we are the ultimate culprits."[3]

U. S. Secretary of the
Interior Bruce Babbitt

5. Amphibian decline has potentially serious consequences for the human race. Babbitt says that he is worried about "the human implications" of amphibian decline. Will whatever is killing amphibians today kill us tomorrow?

6. So far, despite all the work of the scientists in DAPTF and other organizations dedicated to solving the mystery of amphibian decline, we have not been doing an effective job of working together. Babbitt said, "We have a lot of assets and a lot of wonderful research capability in the federal government, but it has not been coordinated and focused on a worldwide attempt to gather the information and understand the causes, which we must do if we're going to respond to the emergency."[4]

7. We must begin working effectively together right now. It is the only way to solve the mystery of amphibian decline. One ecologist, not at the meeting, put it this way: "I want to do something to help save some of these magnificent creatures for my children's children."[5]

A Few Success Stories

One way in which scientists and government agencies are currently cooperating to halt amphibian decline is captive breeding. Amphibians are being bred in captivity and then released into the wild.

The Wyoming Toad Recovery Program is an example. This is a cooperative venture involving the Wyoming Game and Fish Department, the U.S. Fish and Wildlife Service, and several zoos. Together, these organizations saved the Wyoming toad from extinction. By 1994, Wyoming toads had all but disappeared from the wild. Fortunately, eighty remained in captivity and were carefully bred. Since 1994, more than 9,500 tadpoles and toadlets have been reintroduced into their native habitat in the Laramie Basin. This small miracle could not have been accomplished without a great deal of care and planning. Captive-bred tadpoles were carefully placed in protected areas in the basin lake, and allowed to metamorphose into toads. Then they were released into the larger lake. The project has been a tremendous success.

Then there's the biodiversity lab at St. Joseph's University in Philadelphia, Pennsylvania, another successful captive-breeding site. Scientists at the lab have been breeding the South American poison dart frog since their natural habitat in eastern Ecuador was destroyed. The venom of these frogs is used in the production of a potent pain-killing drug (see Chapter 1).

Amphibians are also being bred in captivity by pet suppliers. Singapore and Hong Kong both have booming pet-supply industries. Pet suppliers say that with these captive-bred amphibians readily available for purchase, wild amphibians are less likely to be hunted down and captured. Advocates of captive breeding hope that these efforts will help keep wild amphibians in the wild, where they belong.

Another sign that attitudes toward amphibian decline are changing is an ambitious project taking place in the Great Smoky Mountains. From 1998 to 2002, scientists from the U.S. Geological Survey intend to make an inventory of forty species of amphibians in Great Smoky Mountains

National Park, home to more amphibian species than anywhere else in North America. The researchers will be looking everywhere—behind rocks, inside hollow logs, and under leaf beds. These concerned scientists are responding to the news of worldwide amphibian decline. Their purpose is to keep track of population trends in the Great Smokies and spot any environmental changes before they turn lethal. This is only one of many such surveys of amphibians that scientists are conducting all around the world.

The growth of the DAPTF is another promising sign. In the first 7 years of its existence, DAPTF expanded from 1,200 scientists at work in 30 countries to more than 3,000 scientists at work in more than 90 different countries.

Meanwhile, the mystery of worldwide amphibian decline continues, and we humans continue to wonder why it's taking place and what it will mean for us. "Our lives are intertwined with those of these moist-skinned creatures," says Sam Droege, a biologist with the U.S. Geological Survey. "We breathe the same air and drink the same water. When extinctions occur among species whose roots on this planet surpass ours by millions of years, we should be listening to what they say."[6]

GLOSSARY

acid precipitation—rain, snow, mist, or fog that becomes high in acid content due to human-made chemical pollutants.

anthropologist—a scientist who studies ancient peoples and the artifacts they left behind.

anuran—the group of amphibians that includes frogs and toads. Anurans have no tails.

bacteria—a group of one-celled microorganisms, some of which may cause diseases.

biodiversity—the variety of life on Earth, including all species of plants and animals.

caecilians—the group of amphibians with no legs.

chlorofluorocarbons (CFCs)—human-made compounds that destroy ozone molecules.

cold-blooded—having a body temperature that changes with the surrounding environment.

DDT—dichloro-diphenyl-trichloroethane; a widely used pesticide that has now been banned because it poisons a variety of animals.

decline—to become fewer and fewer, less and less.

DNA—the molecule that carries the genetic code—the instructions that tell a cell how to grow and function.

ecologist—a scientist who studies how organisms interact with their environment.

ecosystem—an area made up of a distinct environment and the organisms that inhabit it, such as a lake, a front yard, or a desert.

embryo—an organism in the early stages of its development.

endangered—in danger of becoming extinct.

environmental degradation—the overall breakdown in the quality and health of everything that affects the development of living things.

enzyme—a protein, produced by living cells, that helps to activate the chemical processes of life.

epidemic—the rapid spread of a disease.

extinction—the process by which a species dies off or disappears from the Earth forever.

fluctuation—in terms of species, the natural rise and fall of a population over time.

food web—a group of organisms in an ecological community that feed upon one another.

fungus—a life form (neither plant nor animal) that gets nourishment from other organic matter.

greenhouse effect—a warming of Earth's surface and lower atmosphere that occurs when gases in the atmosphere trap infrared rays. This process is similar to the way in which glass traps heat in a greenhouse.

habitat—the place in the environment where a particular plant or animal lives and grows.

herpetologist—a scientist who studies reptiles and amphibians.

HIV—human immunodeficiency virus; individuals infected with this virus usually develop AIDS (acquired immune deficiency syndrome).

hormone—a protein that affects the activity of some organ or tissue.

host—the plant or animal on which a parasite depends for food and shelter.

hypothesis—an educated guess; a statement, usually an attempt to solve a problem, that seems true but must be tested in order to be proven true.

immune system—the natural mechanisms used by the body to destroy foreign organisms and particles.

infrared ray—radiation from the invisible part of the electromagnetic spectrum, making up most of the heat from the sun.

larva (pl. *larvae*)—the immature form of an amphibian, such as a tadpole, which must undergo metamorphosis to become an adult.

metamorphosis—the extreme changes an amphibian goes through as it grows from larva to adult.

methoprene—a potent pesticide.

ozone—a molecule present in Earth's stratosphere that reflects ultraviolet rays back into space.

parasite—an organism that lives off other organisms, known as hosts.

pathogen—a disease-causing agent.

permeable—easy for water and air to pass through.

pesticide—a substance used to kill pests, such as insects, rodents, microorganisms, or weeds.

photolyase—an enzyme designed to repair damage from UVB rays in amphibians.

predator—an animal that kills and eats other animals.

prey—an animal that is killed and eaten by other animals.

rain forest—a dense forest in a region where rainfall is heavy all year long.

species—a group of related organisms that have common characteristics and naturally interbreed.

sterile—unable to produce offspring.

toxin—a poison produced by a living organism.

trematode—a microscopic parasitic flatworm.

ultraviolet ray—radiation from the invisible part of the electromagnetic spectrum, present in sunlight.

vertebrate—an animal with a backbone and nervous system.

wetland—an area with extremely moist soil, such as a bog or swamp.

END NOTES

Introduction
1. Yoffe, Emily. "Silence of the Frogs." *New York Times Magazine.* December 13, 1992, p. 36.

2. Yoffe, ibid.

Chapter 1
1. Yoffe, ibid, p. 64.

Chapter 2
1. Friedman, Thomas L. "Mr. Toad's Last Ride." *New York Times.* June 6, 1998, p. A23.

2. Livermore, Beth. "Amphibian Alarm: Just Where Have All the Frogs Gone?" *Smithsonian.* October, 1992, p. 115.

Chapter 3
1. Petit, Charles. "Disappearance of Toads, Frogs Has Some Scientists Worried." *San Francisco Chronicle.* April 20, 1992. In Internet page at URL: <frog.simplenet.com/froggy/sciam/frogs-disappear.txt>.

2. Luoma, Jon. "Vanishing Frogs." *Audubon.* May-June, 1997, p. 63.

3. Gannon, Robert. "Frogs in Peril." *Popular Science.* December, 1997, p. 85.

Chapter 4

1. Petit, ibid.

2. Livermore, ibid.

3. Yoffe, ibid, p. 66.

4. Yoffe, ibid, p. 64.

Chapter 5

1. De Sam Lazaro, Fred. "Freaky Frogs." December 23, 1996. In Internet page at URL <www.pbs.org/newshour/bb/science/july-dec96/frogs_12-23.html>.

2. Gannon, ibid, p. 87.

3. Kaiser, Jocelyn. "Deformed Frogs Leap into Spotlight at Health Workshop." *Science.* December 19, 1997, p. 2052.

4. "Is a New DDT Killing Frogs?" November 20, 1997. In Internet page at URL: <archive.abcnews.com/sections/scitech/frogs930>.

5. Meersman, Tom. "Deformed-Frog Meeting Is Short on Answers, Long on Speculations." *Minneapolis Star Tribune.* April 17, 1997. In Internet page at URL: <www.npwrc.usgs.gov/index.htm archive>.

6. Kroon, Betsy. "Frog Project, Personal Reflection." In Internet page at URL: <www.mncs.k12.mn.us/frog/bkroon.html>. Updated November 15, 1997.

7. Fisher, Ryan. "Mystery of the Frogs." In Internet page at URL: <www.mncs.k12.mn.us/frog/ryan.html>. Updated November 15, 1997.

8. Wellburn, Elizabeth. "Frogs and the Environment: Network Nuggets." In Internet page at URL: <www.etc.bc.ca/cgi-bin/goto/~gateway/nuggets/archives/0019.htm?frogs#first_hit>. Posted October 1, 1997.

9. "Background Information about Deformed Frogs in Minnesota." In Internet page at URL: <www.pca.state.mn.us/hot/frog-bg.html#what>. Updated April 15, 1998.

10.. Souder, William. "Colleagues Say Frog Deformity Researchers Leaped Too Soon." *Washington Post.* November 3, 1997. In Internet page at URL: <www.npwrc.usgs.gov/index.htm archive>.

11. Kaiser, ibid.

Chapter 6

1. Luoma, ibid.

2. Recer, Paul. "UV Radiation Can Be Deadly." December 8, 1997. In Internet page at URL: <archive.abcnews.com/sections/scitech/amphibiansun1208/>.

3 "Is a New DDT Killing Frogs?" ibid.

4. Lips, Karen R. "Recent Amphibian Declines in Lower Central America." *Froglog.* June, 1997. In Internet page at URL: <acs-info.open.ac.uk/info/newsletters/froglog-22.html>.

5. "Frog-Killing Fungus Identified." June 24, 1998. In Internet page at URL: <www.abcnews.com/sections/science/DailyNews/frogfungus980624.html>.

6. Livermore, ibid.

Conclusion

1. Chadwick, Alex. "Decline of Amphibians." *NPR Morning Edition* (transcript). May 19, 1998, p. 12.

2. Chadwick, ibid.

3. Chadwick, ibid., p. 13.

4. Chadwick, ibid., p. 12.

5. Phillips, Kathryn. *Tracking the Vanishing Frogs.* New York: St. Martin's Press. 1994, p. 159.

6. Droege, Sam. "An Outline of Issues Associated with Amphibian Declines." Internet page at URL: <http://www.mp1-pwrc.usgs.gov/amphib/frogsum.html>. Posted May 22, 1998.

SELECTED BIBLIOGRAPY

Beardsley, Tim. "Murder Mystery." *Scientific American.* November, 1991, p. 29.

Blaustein, Andrew. "Amphibians in a Bad Light." *Natural History.* November, 1994, pp. 32–38.

Blaustein, Andrew R. and Wake, David B. "The Puzzle of Declining Amphibian Populations." *Scientific American.* April, 1995, pp. 52–57.

Carey, Cynthia. "Disease, Stress and Amphibian Declines." *Froglog.* June, 1997. Internet page at URL: <acs-info.open.ac.uk/info/newsletters/froglog-22-2.html>.

Conlon, Michael. "Clue Found in Deformed Frog Mystery." *Toronto Star.* November 6, 1996. Internet page at URL: <www.cciw.ca/green-lane/herptox/methoprene.html>.

Chadwick, Alex. "Decline of Amphibians." *NPR Morning Edition* (transcript). May 19, 1998.

De Sam Lazaro, Fred. "Freaky Frogs." December 23, 1996. Internet page at URL: <www.pbs.org/newshour/bb/science/july-dec96/frogs_12-23.html>.

Droege, Sam. "An Outline of Issues Associated with Amphibian Declines." Internet page at URL: <http://www.mp1.usgs.gov/amphib/frogsum.htm>. May 22, 1998.

Friedman, Thomas L. "Mr. Toad's Last Ride." *New York Times.* June 6, 1998, p. A23.

Gannon, Robert. "Frogs in Peril." *Popular Science.* December, 1997, pp. 84–88.

Halliday, Timothy and Heyer, W. Ronald. "The Case of the Vanishing Frogs." *Technology Review.* May/June, 1997. Internet page at URL: <www.techreview.com/articles/mj97/halliday.html>.

Kaiser, Jocelyn. "Deformed Frogs Leap into Spotlight at Health Workshop." *Science.* December 19, 1997, pp. 2051–2052.

Koop, David. "Animals Smuggled in Boxes." August 26, 1997. Internet page at URL: <archive.abcnews.com/sections/world/peru826>.

Lips, Karen R. "Recent Amphibian Declines in Lower Central America." *Froglog.* June, 1997. Internet page at URL: <acs-info.open.ac.uk/info/newsletters/froglog-22.html>.

Livermore, Beth. "Amphibian Alarm: Just Where Have All the Frogs Gone?" *Smithsonian.* October, 1992, pp. 113–120.

Martin, Glen. "Froggy Bottom." *Discover.* May, 1990, pp. 36–37.

Meersman, Tom. "Deformed-Frog Meeting Is Short on Answers, Long on Speculations." *Minneapolis Star Tribune.* April 17, 1997. Internet page at URL: <www.npwrc.usgs.gov/index.htm archive>.

Mlot, Christine. "Water Link to Frog Deformities Strengthened." *Science News.* October 11, 1997, p. 230.

MNCS Frog Project." Internet page at URL: <www.mncs.k12.mn.us/frog/frog.html>. Last updated November 15, 1997.

"Monteverde Golden Toad." Internet page at URL: <http://www.ckmc.com/bagheera/clasroom/casestud/gldntoad.htm>.Posted July 2, 1996.

Pechmann, Joseph, et al. "Declining Amphibian Populations: The Problem of Separating Human Impacts from Natural Fluctuations." *Science.* August 23, 1991, pp. 892–894.

Petit, Charles. "Disappearance of Toads, Frogs Has Some Scientists Worried." *San Francisco Chronicle.* April 20, 1992. Internet page at URL: <frog.simplenet.com/froggy/sciam/frogs-disappear.txt>.

Phillips, Kathryn. *Tracking the Vanishing Frogs.* New York: St. Martin's Press. 1994.

Recer, Paul. "UV Radiation Can Be Deadly." December 8, 1997. Internet page at URL: <archive.abcnews.com/sections/scitech/amphibian sun1208/>.

Sessions, Stanley. "Current Research on Naturally Occurring Deformities in Amphibians." Internet page at URL: <www.hartwick.edu/biology/def_frogs/back/background.html>. Last updated July 12, 1998.

Souder, William. "Colleagues Say Frog Deformity Researchers Leaped Too Soon." *Washington Post.* November 3, 1997. Internet page at URL: <www.npwrc.usgs.gov/index.htm archive >.

Souder, William. "New Report of Deformed Frogs Triggers U.S. Ecological Alarms." *Washington Post.* January 29, 1997. Internet page at URL: <www.npwrc.usgs.gov/index.htm archive >.

Wake, David. "Declining Amphibian Populations." *Science.* August 23, 1991, p. 891.

Yoffe, Emily. "Silence of the Frogs." *New York Times Magazine.* December 13, 1992, pp. 36–38, 64–76.

ONLINE SITES

Would you like to learn more about amphibians and amphibian decline? See the Bibliography section of this book for books and articles.

A great deal of information is also available on the World Wide Web. If you have access to a personal computer that's connected to the Internet, you can use any of the World Wide Web's search engines (Yahoo, Alta Vista, Excite, etc.) to call up lists of Web sites that deal with amphibians. Try some of the following key words:

- amphibians
- frogs
- toads
- salamanders
- caecilians
- wetlands
- global warming
- herpetology
- ozone shield
- acid rain

The following is a list of information-packed Web sites devoted to amphibians and to issues related to amphibian decline. Because Internet sites cannot be permanently stored on shelves like books, they may cease to exist over time. But the sites listed below are reliable and have been in existence for a while now.

Amphibia
http://www.york.biosis.org/zrdocs/zoolinfo/grp_amph.htm
Links to dozens of Web sites devoted to amphibians.

Amphibian Studies WWW Site
http://www.fws.gov/r9endspp/endspp.html
Developed by the Biological Resources Division of the U.S. Geological
Survey. Up-to-date record of U.S. endangered and threatened amphibians,
with detailed technical information on each species.

Atmospheric Radiation Measurement (ARM) Program
http://www.arm.gov/
Click on "Search" and type in "global warming" or "greenhouse effect."
Dozens of articles with diagrams and photographs.

DAPTF Home Pages
http://www.open.ac.uk/OU/Academic/Biology/J_Baker/JBtxt.htm
Home pages of the Declining Amphibians Populations Task Force (see
Chapter 2), including *Froglog*, the DAPTF newsletter.

*Endangered Species Classroom: Monteverde Golden Toad and Other Amphib-
ians*
http://www.ckmc.com/bagheera/clasroom/casestud/gldntoad.htm
Concise summary of causes of amphibian decline. Includes photographs.

Index to Deformed Frog Research
http://www.hartwick.edu/biology/def_frogs/index.html
Click on "Chemicals Versus Parasites" and sample the "Trematodes" and
"Methoprene" links. Includes deformed frog photographs.

MNCS Frog Project
http://www.mncs.k12.mn.us/frog/frog.html
Web site of New Country School in Le Sueur, Minnesota (see Chapter 5).

Northern Prairie Wildlife Research Center
http://www.npwrc.usgs.gov/
Click from "Site Map" to "Biological Resources by Taxon" to "Amphibians and Reptiles" to "Species Identification Guide for Amphibians in the United States and Canada." Includes photographs and detailed descriptions of dozens of amphibian species.

World Conservation Monitoring Center
http://www.wcmc.org.UK/cgi-bin/ct_ap.p
Search this database of extinct and endangered animals worldwide. Click on "Amphibia" under "CLASS name" and select "Threat Categories" and "Country."

The World Wide Web Virtual Library: Herpetology
http://cmgm.stanford.edu/~meisen/herp/
More links, but these are more varied and specialized than the ones in Amphibia. Here you get links, for instance, to sites of captive breeding suppliers, herpetology museums around the world, and employment opportunities in the field of herpetology.

How You Can Help

Would you like to help the scientists working to understand the causes of amphibian decline? If you have access to a personal computer that's connected to the Internet, you can lend a hand by visiting the following sites.

A Thousand Friends of Frogs
http://cgee.hamline.edu/frogs/
This site is designed for K–12 students and educators, aimed at helping frogs to survive and thrive. Inspired by Judy Helgen of the Minnesota Pollution Control Authority (see Chapter 5). Click on "Get involved."

Frog Collecting Guidelines
http://www.mncs.k12mn.us/frog/surveymain.html.
When you look for amphibians, be sure you're not trespassing. Also, make sure you don't harm any wildlife. This site will provide tips for locating, collecting, and keeping amphibians.

North American Reporting Center for Amphibian Malformations
http://www.npwrc.usgs.gov/narcam/
Click on "Where Have Malformations Been Reported" to see reports of frog deformities in your state. Click on "How Can I Submit a Report" to see how you can get involved. Includes pictures of specific types of deformities for identification.

North American Amphibian Monitoring Program
http://www.mp1-pwrc.usgs.gov/amphib/regions/regions.html
Click on your state or province and find out how you can get involved in keeping track of the amphibians in your area.

Chemical Scorecard
http://www.scorecard.org/
This site is sponsored by the Environmental Defense Fund. By typing in your zip code, you can learn about the pollution in your community: how extensive it is and who's doing it. The "Take Action" section details steps you can take to help change the situation.

 INDEX

ABOUT THE AUTHOR

Ron Fridell has been writing since his college days at Northwestern University, where he earned a Master's Degree in radio, television, and film. He has written for radio, TV, newspapers, and textbooks. He taught English as a second language while a member of the Peace Corps in Bangkok, Thailand. He lives in Evanston, Illinois, with his wife Patricia and their dog, an Australian shepherd named Madeline.